Inherited Trauma & Family Wealth

A guide to heal your relationships and build a lasting legacy

RUSCHELLE KHANNA, LCSW

Inherited Trauma & Family Wealth - A guide to heal your relationships and build a lasting legacy © 2024 By Ruschelle Khanna. All rights reserved. No part of this book may be used or reproduced in any manner whatsoever, including internet usage, without written permission from Ruschelle Khanna, except in the case of brief quotations embodied in critical articles, reviews, and cites in professional texts.

First Edition
First Printing 2024

Library of Congress Cataloging-in-Publication Data is on file with the Library of Congress.

Limit of Liability/Disclaimer of Warranty: The author and anyone else involved in creating this book make no representations or warranties with respect to the completeness of the contents of this work and specifically disclaim all warranties, including without limitation warranties of fitness for every situation, despite best efforts to make the work exhaustive. This work does not purport to replace professional help, but can act as an adjunct to professional help. Neither the author nor anyone else involved in the course shall be liable for damages arising from incorrect use of the strategies and techniques outlined in the course book. No warranty may be created or extended by sales or promotional materials. The advice and strategies contained herein may not be suitable for every situation. The work is sold with the understanding that the author is not engaged in this book in offering medical, legal, or other professional advice or services. This book is not meant to be used to diagnose mental health conditions and a professional mental health provider should be contacted if such a diagnosis is required. The fact that an individual organization is referred to in this work as a citation or potential source of further information does not mean the author endorses the information the individual or organization may provide. Further, readers should be aware that websites referenced in this work may have changed or disappeared between when this work was written and when it was read.

Note: Clients' names and circumstances have been changed to protect privacy; any similarities are unintentional and unintended.

Cover Design: Ruschelle Khanna
Developmental Editor: Diane Cady
Editorial Project Manager: Lorretta Smith

ECHO Legacy Press

Printed in the United States of America

Table of Contents

Foreword	iv
Introduction	vi
Part One Where Money Stories Are Held	**1**
Chapter One: Your Body Holds Your Money Story	2
Chapter Two: Echoes of Trauma	11
Chapter Three: Communities of Healing	21
Chapter Four: Building Blocks of the Money Story	29
Part Two Uncovering Inherited Trauma	**42**
Chapter Five: Accounting for Our Relationships	44
Chapter Six: Securities	51
Chapter Seven: Emotional Currency	60
Chapter Eight: Understanding Options	67
Chapter Nine: Social Capital	75
Chapter Ten: Bankruptcy	83
Part Three Creating an ECHO Legacy™	**91**
Chapter 11: One Solution	93
Conclusion	116
Acknowledgements	119
Bibliography	120
RUSCHELLE KHANNA, LCSW	127

Foreword

This book isn't solely about wealth.

Just as money isn't simply about numbers. This book serves as an introduction to exploring your personal money story—one that you have been unconsciously writing and which has also been shaped by past generations. Ruschelle Khanna offers a comprehensive overview of various concepts related to inherited trauma and their impact on a family's relationship with wealth, while also providing actionable steps you can take to address these issues. It is uncommon to find a topic as complex as this one presented with such a tangible framework for understanding how people relate to their finances. Khanna's approach also offers specific tools and paths that can help you work through some of the financial challenges you may be facing. The ECHO model she presents is an especially effective tool for healing inherited financial traumas and can also serve as a broader framework for cultivating nurturing family relationships.

In my work as a financial therapist, I frequently encounter stories similar to those described in this book, and I am grateful to see them shared here. Unfortunately, there are only a limited number of professionals like Ruschelle who possess expertise in both financial matters and mental health. With fewer than 100 financial therapists currently practicing in the country, many of the questions posed in this book may not often be explored unless you have the good fortune of working with one of these specialists. In other words, consider this a valuable opportunity to learn from a true expert!

Ruschelle lays the groundwork for significant personal reflection and growth, which lies at the heart of financial therapy. This is not a book to skim casually; rather, it has the potential to guide you on a transformative journey of self-discovery regarding money and family healing. This journey offers the chance to heal from inherited wounds and develop the skills necessary to leave a different, healthier legacy for the next generation. I strongly encourage you to engage with the questions posed in the book by writing down your responses. Books like this are meant to be thoroughly interacted with, filled with notes, highlights, and insights scrawled in the margins.

Monetary and traumatic inheritance often evoke similar emotions, beliefs, and challenges. However, they can also pave the way for healing, hope, and a more enriching life experience. Your income level or financial assets are secondary—what truly matters is that everyone has a relationship with money. Money acts as a canvas upon which all our traumas, triumphs, and values are reflected, shaping the stories we tell ourselves. None of us have ever experienced money without some emotional context, and Ruschelle Khanna masterfully illustrates just how deeply rooted your money story is. As you delve into understanding your money story and the ECHO framework, you may find that your perspective on money shifts significantly. Ideally, this journey will also lead you to view yourself and your family history in a more insightful, healing light.

Nathan Astle is the Founder of the Financial Therapy Clinical Institute where he provides clinical services in financial therapy and trains clinicians in the discipline. He is a Marriage and Family Therapist and Certified Financial Therapist. He specializes in couples experiencing financial conflict, financial anxiety and financial trauma. He has been featured in numerous outlets like CNBC, USA Today, New York Times, and the Wall Street Journal. He has served as a past board member for the Financial Therapy Association and regularly consults with businesses on implementing financial therapy tools in their work.

Introduction

Many people in my circle, both personal friends and clients, harbor some emotional pain around accumulating and sustaining wealth. Your circle may not be much different. This book addresses some of the sources of that emotional pain and the role generational trauma plays in our ability to accumulate and sustain family wealth. The project was born from years of exploration into the experiences of individuals and families across the socio-economic spectrum, from rural Appalachia to Wall Street. At the heart of my work lies an interest in uncovering the unconscious themes that are usually buried in long held family narratives. These unconscious themes often emerge as the drivers of many of our current decisions... especially surrounding money.

In this book you will:

- Obtain a basic understanding of how inherited trauma affects us as individuals, families and communities.
- Gain an understanding of how the stories we carry from generation to generation impact our behavior with money.
- Be guided through a process of uncovering your unique reactions to inherited trauma.
- Be provided a framework for helping you and your family work through those patterns and learn to establish new ones leading to generational wealth.

But first, an explanation of some terms. What is meant by wealth? What is meant by generational trauma? And how does generational trauma relate to our beliefs and behaviors around wealth?

The *Merriam-Webster Dictionary* provides a standard definition of wealth as "an abundance of material possessions or resources."[70] While that is the textbook definition of wealth, the modern definition is certainly shifting. The old definition, linked to status, possessions, or "keeping up with the Joneses," is one based on insecurity.

This new definition transcends how much money we have and focuses on how our resources work for us. Modern, educated families define wealth through a lens not of lack and status, but rather of security. They ask questions like, "Do my resources support my body, mind, and spirit?"; "Can I afford quality time with my family?"; and "Will my legacy make a better world for my grandchildren?"

For the purposes of this book, my definition of wealth is:

A felt sense of security regardless of circumstances, and feeling resourced in all ways and in all endeavors.

This more expansive definition of wealth includes how resources impact one's goals, including:

1. Health & longevity
2. Desired lifestyle goals including experiences
3. Increased connection to family
4. Philanthropic impact on communities and the planet

We will discuss how inherited patterns of pain and trauma interfere with those goals. But first, it's important to define inherited trauma. Essentially, inherited trauma (also known as intergenerational or ancestral trauma) is the idea your ancestors' trauma can be passed down through generations, impacting your current life experiences and decisions. This inheritance can happen through:

1. Nature - Our genetic material carries information from one generation to another.
2. Nurture - Behaviors passed down through child rearing.
3. Collective Experience - Traumas passed down due to collective experiences in a community or group.

It is not always known, however, if one's family or community has experienced inherited trauma. This book explores three clear signs inherited trauma might be present:

- First, you may legitimately recognize you engage in an unhealthy pattern of behavior, but you do it anyway. If the behavior appears similar to that of even a distant family member or if it is a behavior embedded in your family's culture, it's probably something to explore.

- The second is a behavior you possess with absolutely no idea where it came from or why you do it. After lengthy exploration, possibly years in therapy, you cannot pin it to any experiences occurring in your lifetime. I know this second one to be true because genealogy research has helped uncover uncanny stories from past generations matching the current experiences of clients. But you don't need to start performing intense genealogical research to heal generational patterns (although you can and I have found it life changing for clients). I promise more than enough information exists to move us in a good direction.

- The third one is the most common according to the preeminent inherited trauma clinician Mark Wolynn: the sudden onset of anxiety or fear when we hit a certain age or reach a certain milestone. Wolynn states: "It's as though there's an ancestral alarm clock inside us that starts ringing".[53]

There are a number of pressing reasons why this work is now more important than ever. In particular, right now in the United States, we are living through two cultural tsunamis of which this book aims to consider and influence. One wave deals with the ongoing generational healing and aftermath of the Opioid epidemic which has impacted millions of Americans beyond those directly addicted. The second pertains to the Great Wealth Transfer in which $84.4 trillion will be transferred from baby boomers and the Silent Generation (preceding boomers) to their heirs.[1] Both of these events have sent waves of impact through the families and communities impacted. This book examines current events and historical moments referencing Appalachia as an example of the connection between people and place.

If generations harbor unresolved stories of lack, guilt, and fear, an influx of money does not mean they are suddenly equipped to make and sustain lasting wealth. Due to the massive transfer of wealth from baby boomers to the next generation, an increasing need exists and interest in the ways generational patterns, traumas, and family strengths impact our relationship with money. Many programs are popping up across the country to equip the next generation with tools to succeed in a changing financial landscape. You will meet some of the founders of those programs here. While many books focus on healing financial wounds, as well as setting up better family business dynamics and governance structures, I have yet to see a guide tying the two together. This book is my attempt to do just that. I will provide you with a basic understanding of generational trauma, its impact on money and my framework to provide families with the tools to preserve legacies. I will give examples and clear tools to address the limiting beliefs holding us back from embracing true wealth and passing the experience on to our children and communities.

Today's financial landscape is also shifting. Generational ideas about money and the changing definition of family contribute to a massive disconnect between the ability for families to earn wealth and preserve it for future generations. Understanding trauma helps us appreciate generational fluctuations in emotional and financial security that have nothing to do with money and everything to do with the stories and relationships driving behaviors. The stories of our past can be the unknown, the wildcard in understanding how we, as families and as a society, end up in unsteady financial circumstances. For years it was believed that by the third generation, 70% of family fortunes were lost.[72] Today we know that research to be a bit misleading. In fact, many family advisors cite an increase in family education and awareness around financial education and stewardship. However, with the impact of the Great Wealth Transfer, including more women becoming financial leaders in their households, it continues to be important to learn the impact of deeply held family hurts on our finances. Now more than ever, I observe society's need for a reckoning with regard to relationships, including the one we have with money.

Wealth management is also changing. Technological improvements have rapidly changed how we interact with advisors and our money. Advisors need to evolve to address the more specific and unique needs of their clients, especially women, first time investors (specifically from minority groups), and newly affluent inheritors of wealth.[2] Advisors are now required to explore other ways of adding value. One path the financial industry adds value is by utilizing more financial therapists who help clients understand financial trauma and advocate against racist policies in the financial industry. It is particularly important to understand how generational trauma impacts finances in underserved communities. We know, for example, that Black household income is increasing.[73] However, evidence suggests this increase in income does not always translate into wealth development. One example of change includes an increase in financial therapists helping educate minority communities about the power of investing in minority owned businesses and how they can focus on philanthropy and investments important to them.

You may be approaching this book wondering, "But what if I didn't experience any trauma?". And to that I would say there are two key reasons for reading:

1. Being trauma-informed is a valuable skill regardless of your family status or occupation. The more we know about how those around us respond to trauma, the easier it is to communicate effectively. When we are trauma-informed we can support family, friends and colleagues in a more powerful way.
2. Trauma hides from conscious awareness. My premise is that there may be blind spots in your own history you remain unaware of impacting your decisions around money. This book offers you the opportunity to explore patterns of inherited trauma you may yet recognize.

Parts I and II of the book provide the background and theory of inherited trauma and family wealth. Part I begins with a look at our physiology and its role in one of the most important functions of the brain–making meaning from the world around us. The mind performs this task by creating a story. As adults, early stories drift like a dream into the unconscious and become the autopilot driving our behaviors. In this book we will delve deeper into the stories of the individuals, families and communities shaping our lives. The re-telling of stories results in slight changes with each sharing, and different interpretations occur based on the background and time period of the audience. We may be influenced by echoes from past experiences of relatives we never met. We will explore how information (and possibly even full memories) are passed from each generation through genetics. Ultimately, we will begin to sort through stories, eliminating ones no longer serving us.

It is not enough to simply build a theoretical foundation. We must start digging. In Part II, we begin excavating the buried traumas operating behind our money choices. I will provide my argument for the simple yet profound act of slowing down and spending time exploring family stories either independently or as a family. This section introduces you to the foundation needed to begin uncovering your individual and collective narratives. I'll argue for what I refer to as family audits or dedicated time to explore the narratives shaping your money story. In this part, I provide an assessment I use with individuals and families to understand an overview of factors related to trauma and financial habits.

This book discusses safeguarding you and your family from financial disaster as much as it covers establishing and building wealth. And that is only possible through clear conscious actions on the part of ourselves and our organizations. If unconscious wounds become conscious and nothing else is done, we then make decisions from a hazy lens of shame and guilt, which, in fact, is the definition of traumatic stress. Thus, Part III, "Creating an **ECHO Legacy**™," shares my four pillars for successful legacies: **E**ffective communication, **C**ompassionate decision-making, **H**onoring resources, **O**penness to receive. Part III describes the importance of each pillar as well as examples and exercises for you and your family to use to improve that pillar.

While so far I discussed primarily the impact of trauma on individuals, families, and communities, it is important to recognize that in many of these buried narratives resides stories of resilience and triumph. The way individuals, families and communities think about money is viewed through the lenses of our personal history. And that history includes both resilience and trauma. Generally, when we think about finances and trauma, we tend to consider it in terms of a lack of money. Certainly, such a lack is traumatic. Media especially tends to focus on the issue. Headlines usually include weaponized poverty, the fear of the dwindling middle class, fear of running out of funds for retirement, as well as income disparity based on ethnicity. Those incredibly important topics fail to paint a full picture of the complex relationship we have with money. In the last ten years, I focused on serving affluent clients. The types of challenges arising due to an abundance of finances lead to a different type of suffering. Further investigation reveals challenges with money are rarely about money, but much more about the stories and relationships, often generational, which we internalize and act out.

Reading this book will provide you, your family, and clients the tools to break free from generational patterns of victimhood and lack–while recognizing and celebrating stories of resilience in your family and communities.

Are you ready?

Part One

Where Money Stories Are Held

Chapter One: Your Body Holds Your Money Story

The failures of our parents may become our burden, but it is our choice to continue carrying it onward into the next generation or put it down. My adopted beliefs were my written script for living, and I played it out like a self-fulfilling prophecy. As I moved toward healing, I learned unconscious patterns can change once brought into awareness. - Oriana Allen *(The Truth in Our Scars: Untangling Trauma to Discover Your Secret Self)*

Echoes from the Past

Michael Hallett grew up in a middle-class household in the UK. He remembers the subject of money being something completely taboo. He sensed the financial situation was "not good." His grandparents and parents navigated both world wars, leaving them with only enough mental energy to financially survive. Michael described "stumbling into" the working world with little direction from his family. With a gift for understanding systems, Michael had no problem earning large amounts of money as an international consultant for multinational corporations.

Michael remembered his first substantial paycheck—more money than he'd ever made at one time. It induced a sense of disbelief followed by intense anxiety. He quickly blocked these sensations and went about his life. Michael described a lack of acknowledgement in how much he earned, combined with a lack of appreciation, both of which he now describes as symptoms of trauma manifesting in his relationship with money. In addition, Michael described a lifelong fear of paying taxes, which appeared as a common theme among other family members as well.

As Michael's income increased, his inner world grew more chaotic. During this time, Michael began struggling with addictions. His increasing anxiety culminated in a severe panic attack while on a flight to LAX, Michael's life spiraled into intense anxiety and chronic shame.

Michael began to understand the source of these feelings when he attended a healing workshop and learned that he and his father's personalities proved to be "the worst possible pairing for communication." His father lost his mother as a young boy and was not equipped to communicate compassionately with Michael. The feedback Michael received in the workshop unlocked valuable information about his relationship with his father. It appeared as a gateway to healing long-held family wounds directly related to his addictions, habits of overworking, and lack of respect for money.

Part of the healing included uncovering aspects of his family's history. Michael discovered his great grandfather had been tried for tax fraud, and his mother was conceived at the exact time the family descended into the crisis, scandal, and shame related to the trial.

Is it possible our financial issues scar the very fabric of our bodies? Research suggests yes. Our bodies constantly adapt to outside stimulus primarily for survival. These adaptations can be initiated by both inherited and direct experience of traumatic events. If the body cannot find an outlet for releasing the reactions to stress, it stores stress within our tissues. When trauma is held for long periods of time, unable to be released, it causes toxic stress (as opposed to tolerable stress which is necessary for healthy development).[89] But where exactly does this "toxic stress" reside?

Fascia, the web holding us together
One place that holds the stories we've consciously forgotten is the fascia, one of the important (and misunderstood) systems in our body. When formed in your mother's womb, you consisted of a flat disc of cells referred to as an embryonic disc. From the disc, you folded in on yourself, developing a spinal cord, heart and brain. Your heart and brain once touched, growing side by side. Then, one day, in an instant, they split apart to make the top and middle of the spine. As your tiny body formed, a web of thin tissue called the *fascia* held it conjointly. This fascia remained one unit as you grew into an adult. Today, it is the collagen layer holding your insides together.

But it isn't just a structural net. It is a delicate system that, after many years of research, still remains a mystery. We do know the fascia is very sensitive to physical and emotional stresses. The fascia holds your body's reaction to both joyful and stressful experiences. When treating conditions like chronic pain and fibromyalgia, it is thought to be the primary system needing to be addressed.

When emotional or physical toxic stress persists, the body normalizes these experiences. This "new normal" causes aspects of our body to overwork, including high blood pressure as well as heart rate and digestion issues. Essentially, trauma acts as a communication disruptor for all systems in the body. It disrupts the communication channels regulating our physical, mental and relational health, starting with the physical. It seems as if the body functions in third gear, grinding its wheels, using up too much fuel, despite the potential to be running optimally. It physically disrupts the communication pathways allowing us to survive in the world. When we take a step back and slow down, the connection between the health of our fascial system and how we relate to money becomes clear. Beginning at the cellular level, trauma causes errors in our decision-making out of our survival instinct.

Tied to our day-to-day survival, money directly links to trauma. Trauma rips away our sense of stability and personal power. Money portrays the physical representation of these two qualities. Trauma confuses our perception of money's role in our life. We feel anger at the family business and all the money earned from it because it kept our father away many nights when we were a child. We avoid it because we witnessed our parents' messy divorce, fighting over assets. People take advantage or only want to be around us for our money. Trauma is the reason why individuals with massive amounts of money struggle in these areas. Trauma keeps us in behavior loops because the body knows how to react in these familiar scenarios, and as far as the body is concerned, that's more efficient than breaking patterns. Without proper exploration, we could live a lifetime incapable of understanding why these ineffective behaviors continue. If you are reading this book, some part of you is up for the challenge of learning more about the impact of your thoughts, emotions and bodily sensations regarding your perceptions about money.

Trauma Creates Liabilities

Every physical body responds slightly differently to traumatic stress. And from what I have seen, we all possess one type of response critical to survival at one point in childhood. As children, we develop unique ways to navigate stress. Over time, the strategies chosen tend to become firmly patterned into our nervous system. We then carry those creative patterns into adulthood. Problems arise when the strategies fail to fit our adult lives. In fact, with time, they may transform into liabilities. We need new solutions.

Trauma manifests as different variations of liabilities. Physically, it puts us in an energetic debt, literally stealing our vitality and increasing chances of illness. Emotionally, it manifests as guilt and low self-worth. Socially, it steals our ability to connect in a loving and safe way. And financially, it clouds our ability to make healthy decisions to care for our resources. In order to uncover new solutions, we need to understand our nervous system's go-to responses, which again are not "bad," but rather, outdated. The impact of trauma on family legacy devastates not just relationships but business stability, individual ability to care for resources, and continued suffering into the next generation.

Epigenetic impact on daily life

Let's examine Michael's family history of financial devastation and the possible impact on him. Could the stress of tax fraud, including his family's very public humiliation, imprint on Michael's mother, transfer to her children, and thereby impact their beliefs about money? Is this just too far of a stretch? While we tend to think of our financial decisions as behavior we consciously control, that may not be the case. When we investigate the epigenetic impact combined with other factors, such as learned behaviors passed through parenting, we start building a much stronger argument for the connection.

Indeed, the study of inherited trauma indicates a strong possibility. One main component requires understanding epigenetics. Epigenetics is "the study of how your behaviors and environment can cause changes that affect the way your genes work."[6] Inherited trauma plays an important role in epigenetics because it modifies our DNA, informing which genes to "switch on and off." Extremely adverse experiences suffered by our ancestors can shape our health, mental well-being and possibly even specific behaviors.[6] Renowned trauma researchers Rachel Yehuda and Amy Lehrner provided the modern foundational research about inherited trauma and epigenetics. Their 2018 *World Psychiatry* article states:

> Intergenerational trauma acknowledges that exposure to extremely adverse events impact individuals to such a great extent that their offspring find themselves grappling with their parents' post-traumatic state. [And that] … the experience of trauma – or more accurately the effect of that experience – is "passed" somehow from one generation to the next through non-genomic, possibly epigenetic mechanisms affecting DNA function or gene transcription.[6]

Inheriting Memories

> One of the reasons I decided to write this book was discovering that one of my earliest childhood memories is not my own, but my mother's. Beginning around age four, I woke up most nights with terrors, imagining my father died suddenly. I would stay up at night, watching my parents sleep. When he left for his night shift as a local newspaper pressman, I sat by the window in tears, imagining him dead in the front yard. There was no immediate explanation for this fear. It wasn't until I began studying trauma in my graduate education that I realized my four-year-old experience may have actually been linked to my mother's childhood. At age four, my mother's father died suddenly, at home. She was in the front yard at the time of his death. This left my grandmother to raise three children with no income. My mother's trauma became my own. Could that be true?

Inheriting memories is becoming a popular research topic in epigenetics. Along with researchers at Columbia University, Odod Rechavi studies the *C elegans* worm to better understand inheritance of memories. The body is composed of two types of cells: somatic cells (cells that run the body, like blood cells and neurons) and germ cells (sperm and egg). It was once believed that only germ cells transmit information to the next generation. For example, there is a current theory called the soma-to-germline barrier, which posits that changes in your everyday body (soma) cells do not affect your reproductive cells and are not passed onto future generations. However, Rechavi theorizes that RNA molecules (a copy of your dna that leaves the nucleus) could possibly move from the soma cells to the germ cells. Rechavi's study showed that RNA transfers important information, **including memories,** in the C elegans for survival into the third to fifth generations. Rechavi clarifies this study has only shown the transfer of memories in worms, not yet in humans. However, he points out that the results proven about smaller organisms to have later been supported in humans as well. Rechavi states: "If memories are inherited also in humans it might mean you have a greater responsibility for your actions... Regardless of where memory can be inherited in humans or not, it's probably a good idea to act as if it does."[54]

Science is Finally Catching Up

> With Rechavi's worm studies, science is beginning to catch up with the ideas of indigenous cultures. According to LeManuel 'Lee' Bitsoi, Navajo, PhD Research Associate in Genetics at Harvard University, during his presentation at the Gateway to Discovery conference in 2013: Folks in Indian country wonder what took science so long to catch up with traditional Native knowledge. 'Native healers, medicine people and elders have always known this and it is common knowledge in Native oral traditions'.[7]

While worm studies forge a new path for epigenetics and trauma, the research on humans and inherited trauma clearly indicates the experiences of the mother make a significant impact on offspring. Children of mothers who experienced childhood trauma show increased risk for developing behavioral and psychiatric problems. It was previously believed this increased risk arose from the traumatized mother's inability to parent with compassion. However, new evidence indicates babies of mothers who experienced childhood abuse experienced significant changes in brain development, including reduced grey matter.[90]

That does not mean a person whose mother experienced trauma cannot overcome this inheritance. Both Michael and I used curiosity and a lifetime of self-reflection to better understand the impact of our mothers' experiences on our own lives. Both our healing journeys relied heavily on listening to the body sensations we received as we uncovered difficult memories. In the following sections, we are going to explore further how our bodies, not just our minds, hold the keys to thriving in all areas of life.

Trauma is a sneaky thing, in part because it is held in the fascia (the web of tissue holding our bodies together) and the unconscious. Unraveling the complexities of healing requires a desire to better understand how we relate to our bodies, our families, and our resources. How does one uncover these stories? One way, as Michael did, begins with listening to the reactions of one's body to thoughts regarding money and power, emotions like insecurity and lack, and triggers, such as work stress, unexpected bills, and financial conversations.

To begin to unravel the impact of inherited trauma we must deepen the relationship between mind and physical experience. The entry into unraveling inherited trauma can start from many points: the study of genealogy, beginning a mindfulness practice, conversing with our parents, or yoga, and other body-oriented therapies. Even starting an exercise routine sometimes unlocks patterns we never knew we held. This book primarily focuses on building a curiosity toward personal, family, and community stories. Curiosity helps the systems of our body feel safe in the world, allowing us to heal, which in turn, frees up energy to heal everything from physical illness to destructive decision-making.

Industry Expert Insight

> *Traumatized people chronically feel unsafe inside their bodies: The past is alive in the form of gnawing interior discomfort. Their bodies are constantly bombarded by visceral warning signs, and, in an attempt to control these processes, they often become expert at ignoring their gut feelings and in numbing awareness of what is played out inside. They learn to hide from their selves. -Bessel van der Kolk*

The chart on the next page summarizes how traumas from grandparents can impact us to the third generation. Over the next two chapters, we will use versions of this chart to explore inherited traumas' impact on not just individuals but the family system and the community.

INDIVIDUAL ECHOES OF TRAUMA

FIRST GENERATION → SECOND GENERATION → THIRD GENERATION

First Generation
- PTSD due to war
- Participant in or victim of war
- Alcoholism
- Overworking due to extreme poverty
- Abandon of culture due to immigration/discrimination
- Victim of abuse or neglect
- Perpetrator of financial abuse

Second Generation
- Abandonment wounds
- Addictions as coping
- People pleasing
- Cycles of chaos in relationships
- Attachment disorders
- Anger issues
- Challenges managing money
- Intimacy issues
- Obsessive work habits
- Parenting challenges
- Boundary issues

Third Generation
- People Pleasing
- Aversion to marriage and parenting
- Obsessive habits
- Excessive unexplained guilt
- Unstable relationships
- Depression
- Inability to work due to chronic illness

Chapter One Worksheet
"You are the most important person in the room... and so am I."

I often make this statement in therapy as a reminder to clients. They usually respond with confusion. How can we both be the most important? Their question implies it is impossible to hold two conflicting ideas at the same time. Not true. In fact, it is a key indicator of a healthy mind. The ability to do so is called dialectical (or *both/and*) thinking.

The idea that both you and I equally matter is, in my opinion, the most important one in any relationship. It implies we can both be safe and taken care of here in our work together.

The purpose of this chapter was to emphasize that **you** possess a unique way of responding to your inherited and learned experiences. Your health, fulfillment and well-being prove critical to your financial well-being and your ability to sustain and pass down wealth. Therefore, it's very important we start with you. Let's explore some questions just about you.

Reflective Questions
Money Memories

What are your earliest memories of money?

What are the earliest lessons you remember about how to relate to money?

Did your family have sayings about money? If so, what were they?

Do you sense that you have any thoughts or behaviors about money which may not have started with you?

Character Strengths
Name positive money habits or traits you inherited from your family.

What are some strengths you gained due to family hardships?

What do you think is your best quality as a person?

Personal Satisfaction
How satisfied are you in your relationship with money?

How strong is your sense of purpose?

Are there any aspects of your financial life that make you anxious or depressed?

How confident are you in finances and career?

How motivated are you to take care of your overall well-being, including your financial health?

Write down any significant insight you had from reading the chapter and answering the questions above.

Chapter Two: Echoes of Trauma

Our family is an energy field within which we are held, each in our own unique position from the time we are born… Held in this field we are both unconscious and ignorant of its influence… however we are not caught up helplessly in this destiny but can achieve healing.
- Joy Manne, *Family Constellations*

The Body of the Family
Family systems channel tremendous power that can be used as an influential force out into our communities. They also hold tremendous power over us as individuals. The energy of our family body shapes so many of our decisions as adults. Sometimes, this massive amount of energy is directed in harmful ways, not only to others but to the family system itself. The root of this disruption is inherited trauma. Because families are made up of individuals, trauma sends ripples through the family unit by damaging the way we relate to one another. In this chapter, we explore trauma's impact on the body of the family. We will also look at harmonious family dynamics and two main areas of struggle I've witnessed in families living with trauma. Before we wrap up, we will better understand how inherited trauma relates to that often unspoken family influence–money.

The Purpose of the Family
Historically, the purpose of families was successful child-rearing. Once children were old enough, they learned to take over roles necessary for family survival. Throughout history, family and enterprise have been intimately woven together with the goal of collecting resources to properly grow and nurture children. Over the centuries, the successful family team has been of utmost importance.

Industry Expert Insight

> The history of family business is the story of human civilization. A family is the social and economic unit of species survival. In order to nurture, protect, and launch children, the family had to provide security and a livelihood as well as teach children to survive into adulthood. Part of that teaching was sharing the parents' work experience—how to hunt or farm and how to develop skills to produce something valuable toward trade. Every family was also a family business, in that livelihood was a family activity. Every family was a business by necessity.91 Dennis Jaffe, author of Borrowed from Your Grandchildren: The Evolution of 100-Year Family Enterprises

I raise the historical concept of family and enterprise to highlight the fracture modern life caused in the idea of a healthy, well-functioning family team. Unlike today, Jaffe's historical narrative shows no separation between work life, financial stability, and relationship dynamics within the family system. It was expected that family members would find some form of harmony and focus on the collective needs of the family. For example, some earlier societies supported women working and being entrepreneurial and enterprising in a way that put child-rearing first. Society encouraged work in the fields or in collectives with other women in roles allowing for caregiving. This scenario differs greatly from today's expectations of mothers. Unlike many historical examples, the majority of modern society is not supportive of the kinds of teamwork families actually need. Society is no longer set up in a way for parents to be both industrious and present for their children, especially in the most crucial years of development. How exactly do we return to fostering healthy family teams? What makes families motivated and confident to continue functioning together? For this, we look to understand and strengthen the attachments within those families.

Attachments, Trauma, and the Family System

Attachments form in the early stages of life, beginning in utero and if wounded, can contribute to a core element of inherited trauma. Whatever happens to mommy happens to the baby. Because of this we need to understand a bit about attachment theory. Attachment theory was first described by child developmental psychoanalyst John Bowlby. He spent time researching the importance of maternal nurture as it relates to behavior throughout the lifespan. Bowlby emphasized the tremendous impact early secure attachments play in childhood development and in ensuring mentally healthy adults. He demonstrated that infants placed in an unfamiliar situation and separated from their parents will generally react in one of the following ways upon reunion with primary caregivers:

1. Secure attachment: Infants have minimal distress and are easily soothed.
2. Anxious-resistant attachment: A smaller portion of infants experienced greater levels of distress. They seemed to both seek comfort and try to "punish" the caregiver.
3. Avoidant attachment: Infants in the third category showed no stress or minimal stress upon separation and also ignored the caregiver upon their return.[92]
4. Disorganized-disoriented attachment style: These children have no predictable pattern of attachment behaviors.[74]

Some ways our attachment style can be wounded include:

1. Factors causing caregivers to show up inconsistently (especially from ages 0-3). This can include the loss, death or incarceration of a primary caregiver. There is also research on the overuse of daycare as an example of inconsistent

caregiving in early development.[93]
2. Factors preventing caregivers from meeting the child's basic needs. This can include a caregiver with a history of abuse and neglect who is limited in their ability to nurture. Also, mothers who experience anxiety and mood disorders often struggle to keep up with the demands of parenting.

Other factors include divorce, domestic violence, physical illness, and substance abuse.[75] Wounds to these attachment styles can create family disruptions. The most painful wound associated with attachment disorders is the isolated abandonment which might arise from an emotionally absent parent. This can often translate into young adults abandoning the family system altogether. Another challenge related to attachments includes trusting individuals outside the family network who might not be trustworthy in an effort to seek acceptance, leading to being taken advantage of. An example I often see is putting trust in friends who financially take advantage or going into business ventures based on emotions versus due diligence. Other behavioral traits include an overall lack of empathy, poor eye contact, and an inability to regulate emotions, all leading to poor communication.[75] But how exactly does this translate into money issues? In my practice I see two primary ways attachment issues impact our relationship with money, The first involves the impact of family conflict on decision-making related to financial conversations, including developing a will or succession plan. If family members feel abandoned or left out of the decision-making process, they may sabotage the proceedings. Another common way attachment disorders impact money is our personal relationship with it. If we see money as something to be neglected, our finances suffer and we are left uneducated about vital decisions that could protect our assets.

As adults, knowing the four attachment styles can shed light not only on how we interact with our families, but also how we behave regarding issues related to money. In the simplest terms, any attachments other than "secure" results in some form of communication disruption in families (and with financial advisors). Possibly, your family engages in conflict and power struggles when money conversations occur. Or perhaps, you are like the majority of families I have worked with: you simply never speak of anything related to money until a crisis. Understanding attachment styles and resolving issues resembling non-secure attachment is the beginning of a strong family team and easier conversations surrounding money.

A person's attachment style can be greatly impacted by inherited trauma. If we take a look at the Family Echoes of Trauma Chart below, we can see how inherited trauma echoes across generations. With each new generation, it may morph and take on a different variation or shape. The morphing occurs through one primary function of the family system–attachment. For example, if a mother is an alcoholic, unable to provide emotional safety for her daughter, the child may experience abandonment wounds leading to a marriage with a physically abusive husband. This in turn leads to children who may grow up and leave the family system completely.

FAMILY ECHOES OF TRAUMA

FIRST GENERATION	SECOND GENERATION	THIRD GENERATION
• Family wealth gained through exploitation • Loss of wealth due to war • Culture of overworking • Abandon of culture due to immingration/discrimination • Forced separation • Commiting acts of fraud	• Inversion of trust/ lack of trust in family system • Patterns of addiction • Cycles of chaos in relationships • Financial abuse between members • Exploitation from family advisors • Culture of overworking • Absent parent • Boundary issues	• Fractured connections • Aversion to marriage and parenting • Avoidance of family interactions • Excessive unexplained guilt • Unstable relationships • Dwindling financial resources

The Broken Family

It is important to understand attachment styles and their impact because they have a profound influence on trauma and its inheritance. The fact that families experience stressful events is not what causes trauma. Families prove to be super resilient systems, continuing to function despite tremendous barriers in their attachments and treatment of one another. It is actually how individual members respond to traumatic events that causes pain points to emerge in family systems. Like our physical bodies, these pain points cause pain loops that, until released, persist in the family system. In describing "stuck trauma" in the body, recall the amazing system of fascia holding your body together described in Chapter One. The fascia develops knots and "stuck points" when injured, causing tremendous discomfort. The family body is no different. If there is a wound, a betrayal or an abandonment, the family body may respond with tension. In family systems, that tension looks like two things: trauma bonds and inversions of trust.

The Stickiness of Trauma Bonds

Just as individual traumas stick in our bodies, trauma also tends to goo-up in family systems. The reason for this is the relational feedback loop of the trauma bond. A trauma bond develops when an abusive relationship becomes cyclical. It includes patterns of reward as well as emotional attachment toward the abuser. Trauma bonds occur between parents and children, friends, and couples, as well as far more severe power imbalances, including cults and hostage situations.[55] Couples may be trauma-bonded to each other, the patterns of abuse may bounce back and forth with each partner alternating between the role of abuser and victim. Let's take a look at an example of a married couple, Eli and Karen.

Case Study: Cycles of Chaos in Communicating

Karen and Eli have the same argument every week over Eli's financial decisions, how he manages his family's trust, and Karen's overall sense that she is not treated fairly in her marriage. Inevitably, Karen ends up enraged and Eli shuts down emotionally, appeasing Karen with whatever she wants. Karen feels as though she must fight for any form of respect. Eli ends the interaction feeling resentful and powerless. More than likely, these patterns of interacting did not just start in their relationship. They probably glimpsed this dynamic in past romantic relationships or with/between their parents. This conflict loop occurs when traumas are left unresolved. You see, trauma just wants to replay itself and find actors in your life to fill in roles. It wants to keep repeating. By repeating, it hopes for resolution. But without understanding and compassion, the resolution never comes... and the cycles continue.

These patterns of interacting are not "bad"; rather, they are outdated family liabilities no longer contributing to growth. If families overcome trauma bonds, they have found the resources necessary to cultivate the most fulfilling relationships possible, to create the best teams and achieve the best results as a family. At the heart of healing Karen and Eli's cycle, trust is key. Let's dive deeper into understanding trust in family systems.

The Inversion of Trust

Have you known family members who treated strangers better than family for either justified or unjustified reasons? This behavior is often a trauma response; the outcome of which is devastating to families. I refer to this as "The Inversion of Trust." The inversion of trust occurs when we unconsciously deny our family unit. This plays out in very real ways such as neglect, disregard, lack of respect, and at its worst, complete abandonment. This scenario is not an unfamiliar one. In families who experienced a lineage of traumatic events, often an inverted pattern occurs where we disregard our family and put the opinions and needs of outsiders above those closest to us. For the purposes of wealth accumulation and family longevity, this is extremely problematic. In order to begin this discussion, I can't think of a better guide than speaker, author, and entrepreneur, Octavian Pilati.

Pilati's family history reads like the pages of the best historical fiction novel. With its fantastical success and devastating losses, the aristocratic heritage of his family and its enterprises have a history dating back to 1000 AD. When it comes to legacy and survival, they've just about seen it all. One of the most challenging times in Pilati's family history entailed navigating WWII.

While interviewing Pilati, he stated:

> *WWII happened. Most male family members fought and all came back with PTSD. Then we lost our wealth for about ten years because our estates were occupied by the Russians. My father grew up the first ten years of his life in complete poverty... Our estates were then given back when the Russians left Austria. This is still an impact that can be seen in the family today.*

Pilati's family experienced its share of toxic patterns stemming from WWII. For example, survivors of WWII often struggled with alcoholism as a way to cope, leaving their children to suffer the pains of an alcoholic parent. He explains that toxic patterns continue in families when children witness their parent's attempts at coping. Sometimes this coping includes feelings of betrayal and distrust of caregivers or siblings.

Pilati's entry into young adulthood and family business succession coincided with a severe breach of trust—a devastating fraud case struck the family business. The impact of a financial trauma such as fraud within families causes ripples of distrust, shame, and anger throughout the family system. Luckily, Pilati's upbringing and personal genetic makeup proved resourceful enough to overcome these patterns. Pilati's character and background propelled him to be a leader in restoring the family business from tragedy. Pilati also spent time working on his own healing and personal development from his feelings associated with the impact of the financial trauma.

Financial Trauma & The Family

It is important to note that like the examples of war related trauma above, traumas do not have to be directly financial to impact money relationships in families. Trauma permeates parts of our lives we consciously cannot comprehend as related. For example, someone's father may have been in a car accident leaving them fearful of driving. Because of this, the child may learn it isn't safe to take risks, thereby making them risk averse in all areas of life, including investing. The unconscious doesn't care if it rationally makes sense. It just wants the quickest solution to help us find safety. And while those answers made sense in a crisis, they are not always rational or relevant in our current lives. Now that you have an understanding of the leaps and seeming feats of randomness trauma can take, let's examine some more concrete examples.

While some traumas impact finances from an indirect route, others are direct. Family money traumas may be instances of financial abuse, as in the case of Michael's family and his grandfather's tax evasion. Another example of a financial trauma I often see in prominent families is when wealth was acquired from unethical means. Sometimes, family members are completely ashamed of the way their families have used money, including weaponizing it against family members, perpetuating poverty in the communities of their employees, or destroying the environment for economic gain. The shame felt by ancestors around these issues may cause a need to detach from the family in some way. In an interview with Mark Wolyn, author of *It Didn't Start With You: How Inherited Family Trauma Shapes Who We Are and How to End the Cycle*, Wolyn states:

When an ancestor has been unethical or has harmed someone, there is an impulse for descendants to disown or disconnect from this perpetrating ancestor. In my experience, doing so can increase the likelihood of traumatic repetition, in which the descendant can unconsciously repeat the very behavior they condemn. I find that acknowledging this ancestor and his harmful behavior, without cutting off from him, is a healthier direction. In that sense, we acknowledge what happened in the past, and leave the traumatic residue with those who experienced it. Then we turn toward our future, taking the strength we gained from exploring the shadows in our own family history.[5]

Other family money traumas result from victimization due to greed or societal events. These include: surviving the Great Depression, slavery, war, and forced immigration. These catastrophes lead to a number of coping mechanisms in the survivor, resulting in a loss of empathy or a resilience to survive. Genealogist and military researcher Jennifer Holik, helps families explore the impact of World War II on their families. One of her lectures is entitled "Why was Grandma So Mean?" In this lecture, Holik opens up a discussion about the challenges faced by previous generations and how cultivating empathy for these experiences heals the family system. Unfortunately, because some of these experiences resulted in fractures in the family system (such as neglect or abuse), later generations are often left with anger. When I interviewed Mark Wolynn, he explained: "When family members lead unhappy lives or suffer an extremely difficult fate, it's often easier to reject them than to feel the pain of loving them. Anger is often an easier emotion to feel than sadness." The intergenerational anger results in patterns continuing to harm families in innumerable ways: from internalizing criticism leading to low self-worth, addictions, or domestic violence. For subsequent generations, families live with legacies of trauma repeating from one generation to the next.

Now that we have developed an understanding of what inherited trauma can do to the family system including damage to core attachments, repetitive trauma bonds, and inversions of trust, we are ready to explore the larger impact of community. Chapter Three explores the interplay between community trauma, the family, and the individual. But before we move on, feel free to take time to pause and reflect on the questions at the end of this chapter about your family's unique history and experiences with trauma, teamwork, and money.

Chapter Two Worksheet
Family doesn't have to be perfect; it just needs to be united. -unknown

The above quotation is one of my favorite ways to frame family dynamics. The purpose of a family is to protect and support each other. Conflict will be inevitable; it's how the family handles conflict that matters.

Remember the both/and idea from Chapter One? This idea is critical when addressing family pain. We don't have to be in a power struggle. Everyone can get their needs met.

This chapter emphasizes that **your family** possesses a unique way of responding to inherited and learned experiences. The health, fulfillment, and well-being of the family unit prove critical to generational financial well-being. Therefore, we must look at how the family interacts. Let's explore some questions about your family dynamics.

Your Family System Exploration
Do you consider your family a team?

Does your family have a mission and values?

If so, what are they?

What role do you play within your family? Is that role clear?

What were your earliest childhood days like?

What about those of your parents? Grandparents?

Were caregivers present? Worked a lot?

Who would you say you were most attached to?
Can you pick your attachment style from the list?

What are some family stories about money you remember being told?

What is your earliest understanding of your family's economic and financial status in the community?

Were there family secrets around money? If so, what were they?

Were there obvious signs of chaos due to finances?

Did your family consciously teach you how to relate to money?
If so, what were the lessons learned?

List the events in your family history which may have impacted family views on money.

Write down any significant insight you had from reading the chapter and answering the questions above.

Chapter Three: Communities of Healing

Every person is defined by the communities she belongs to. - Orson Scott Card

Our Community Body

As we learned in Chapters One and Two, our physical body is held together by a web of proteins called fascia. We rely on our fascia to be healthy and without "knots" in order for our body to communicate with itself, process emotions, and stay out of pain. We also learned the family is an energy body passing attitudes, behaviors, and relationship patterns between its members. The communities we participate in are no different. They hold a history, stories, and a certain energy unique to that community.

When we define community our first thought might be to refer to the neighborhood in which we live. In reality, an individual may belong to many different communities and these days, the communities may overlap or exist independently from the physical neighborhoods in which we reside. Community can be our religious or professional affiliation, ethnicity, recreational interest, or political affiliation. Often, it is a complex combination of these. Sometimes the combinations of communities cause us to challenge our values, especially in times of hardship. For the purpose of this book we will use Toby Lowe's definition. Lowe, a visiting professor in public management at the Centre for Public Impact in London, states that community is a group of people who share an identity forming narrative.[9] According to Lowe, community narratives play an important role because they form key aspects of individual personalities. In essence, the community history becomes members' personal history. Defining communities in this way aids social change, as we know, re-writing personal narrative creates healing in individuals and the same applies to communities. When we change narratives, whole communities can heal as well.

The influence of community narrative on the individual is the reason why it is impossible to look at family systems without looking at the impact of community traumas on those systems and vice versa. Individuals and families make up our local communities. Like a wave, whatever happens financially within the family system ripples out into main street economies. If communities suffer collective devastation, the impact is felt at home. For example, traumatic events, such as the aftermath of COVID, current international conflicts, and political differences are community stresses that can cause major division within not just the body of the family but the body of the community as well.

In this chapter, we will explore the historical context of financial trauma in the United States. While reading through some of the examples, it is important to remember there are ancestors on both sides of the economic spectrum, both perpetrator and victim, who struggle with the events of the past. In taking a look at the past we realize that although many people benefitted from the suffering of others throughout history, the impact of exploitation will eventually impact all sides in the end. Although it may not be our generation who pays emotionally, when we participate in creating community trauma, it may very well impact the next. With that, let's begin with a trip back in time to a location very relevant to this topic and dear to my heart, central Appalachia.

The Rise and Fall of Little New York

Once referred to as "Little New York," the town of Welch, West Virginia was the world's largest coal producer. Historically, it was known for a community narrative centered around a strong work ethic. Included in the narrative was a unique pocket of support, safety, and entrepreneurship that existed for the Black community residing in Welch. It also carries some of the most intense events of community trauma based on corporate and governmental oppression in the country. One of the worst tragedies to happen on U.S. soil occurred in the neighboring counties: Mingo, Boone, and Logan. In 1920, coal miners attempted to strike for fair wages. The coal companies, backed by the federal government, reacted violently, resulting in the battle of Blair Mountain. It was the first time in U.S. history that the U.S. military dropped bombs on its own citizens.

More recently, a local bank in Welch went from "the most profitable community bank in the country" to "one of the top 10 most costly bank failures in U.S. history".[56] The scandal that was uncovered in 1999– a nationwide fraud scheme–destroyed investments and the town's economy and has been called a "Harbinger of the 2008 Financial Crisis."[56] Compared to other communities in the U.S., Welch has experienced a number of tragedies over the years. Today, the 1700 people living in Welch, WV are still full of stories and pride for what their community once was. However, they struggle to define a primary economy. Drug use among working-age adults in Welch is nearly three times higher than the national average. The life expectancy of someone living in McDowell County is 69 while the national average is 77. Nine percent of the population holds an advanced degree. Employed individuals commute over one hour to and from work per day. The median household income is $30k.[10] And most recently, a third wave of trauma overtook Welch: the opioid epidemic.

A number of factors contributed to the economic and cultural decline of the community. The primary reasons for the community's inability to thrive into the decades beyond coal production include:

- The lack of corporate and national responsibility and reconciliation from war on its citizens.

- The limitations on planning for catastrophic financial events due to oppression.
- Inability to diversify industries outside of coal mining.
- Lack of attention on the health and wellness of community members.
- Lack of infrastructure for higher education for community members.

After reading the example of Welch and the surrounding communities, take a look at the Community Echoes of Trauma chart below. What comes to mind for you as you reflect on the waves of hardship those communities suffered in the form of mass migration, natural disasters, and environmental exploitation? Now think about your community. What tragedies does its history hold? How might these events impact the way individuals view money?

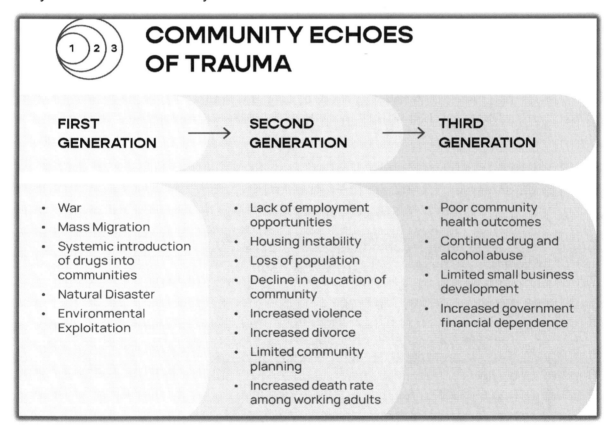

As we can see from the chart, adverse experiences impact more than individuals and families. Communities share their own collective traumas, causing a behavioral feedback loop between them and their members. The economic impact of these events is clear.

Community & Entitlements

Welch is only one example of trauma caused by community exploitation. If you think about the communities you are a part of, I would imagine you can also point to difficult events impacting those communities collectively. One example of financial trauma we continue to contend with in the U.S. is its long and tumultuous history of financial inequality toward minority populations. For example, according to a 2015 article written in *Aeon Magazine* by Professor of American History, Claudio Staunt, *"Between 1776 and the present, the United States seized some 1.5 billion acres from North America's native peoples, an area 25 times the size of the United Kingdom"*.[13]

Staunt describes the less-than-equitable dealings the United States government used to steal native lands:

U.S. title to the land depends on legal fiction, crafted by the colonists to benefit themselves. Under the 'Doctrine of Discovery', which had its origins in the Crusades and underpinned the pioneering navigators of the 15th century, ultimate sovereignty over any pagan land belonged, courtesy of the Vatican, to the first Christian monarch who discovered it. Embraced by imperial powers around the world, the doctrine was adopted by the U.S. Supreme Court in 1823. The U.S. did not rely on Papal Bulls alone, however. It also extinguished the land title of the continent's first peoples by treaty, executive order, and federal statute... Negotiated under duress or facilitated with bribes, treaties were often violated soon after ratification, despite the language of perpetuity.[11]

At the same time President Lincoln entered the Civil War (ostensibly to free the slaves), he simultaneously reduced Native lands nationally by 270 million acres, not by payment or negotiation but by executive order.[76] The story of extending rights to one group while simultaneously taking them away from another is the type of mafia-esque behavior I believe we'd all love to see a bit less of with regard to issues of identity and wealth distribution.

The generations-long exploitation embedded in the American financial system predates the massacre and subsequent land acquisition of Native peoples. Almost 70 years earlier, November 30, 1711, the Common Council of New York City established the slave market in lower Manhattan.[12] It is important to note slaves literally built the "wall" on Wall Street and America's first bond market was backed by slave labor.[13] This is an important fact to consider when communities enter into discussions around healing and the best path forward such as the debate around reparations.

Noting historical events such as the history of the bond market point to the direct connection between discriminatory practices in American finance. More recent practices include charging higher interest rates and redlining, which is to refuse a loan or insurance to someone because they live in an area deemed to be a poor financial risk.[14] Practices such as these have made some members of minority groups distrustful of the financial industry. They are sometimes reluctant to engage in quality financial advising as a consumer and are also hesitant to enter the field as a professional.[15]

Despite distrust in the financial system, financial growth continues to occur in the Black middle class.[17] And with it has come an emphasis on the need for healing and reconciliation around how the Black community relates to money. There has been an influx of thoughtful financial therapists trying to tackle this issue. *Forbes'* contributor Janice Gassam Asare describes the three ways intergenerational trauma impacts the Black community.[18] These three outcomes, while unique in the slave experience, are also echoed in the inherited trauma research from Native communities as well.

1. Slavery results in the phenomenon of low self-esteem, which includes learned helplessness. Asare writes: *Learned helplessness is the perception that no matter what a person does, they cannot change their situation or condition. A person who feels learned helplessness, though frustrated, will stop trying to change their circumstances.* Applied to finances this is a very dangerous concept. My clinical practice has shown this to be the root cause of inability to hold on to savings, leading to compulsive and wasteful spending outside of core values.

2. Asare also cites chronic health challenges in communities historically impacted by mass trauma. Research clearly links chronic health outcomes to lower earning power and financial instability.[69] Poor health outcomes are also shown in Native communities including an increase in metabolic disorders such as diabetes and hypertension and alcoholism.

3. Lastly, Asare cites intergenerational trauma as a cause for internalized oppression. Internalized oppression is the denial of one's own ethnic community, a type of collective self-hate. Internalized oppression disables a community's ability to support itself. It creates an environment where no one is permitted to get ahead and everyone must continue to suffer. These unconscious self-destructive patterns can lead to an inability for families to work together toward financial goals.

What happens when whole communities struggle with self-esteem, chronic health issues, and self-hate? As we explored in Chapter One, the impact results in less energy to take care of oneself, to heal, to be creative, and to push personal limits. Chapter

Two demonstrated the impact results in broken relationships and the inability to work as a team. Communities rely on healthy, thriving members who work well together. The resulting impact on communities manifests as decreased productivity (including earning power), a reduced sense of identity and cultural connection as well as a need for dependence on something other than themselves. This sense of dependence (which at its worst is learned helplessness) is what I believe is a core area to be addressed in communities and families today on both sides of the power divide. In sorting out how these events might still impact us today, one word stands out in my practice above others—entitlements.

When we discuss the word "entitlements" in the context of low-income families, there are arguments for both sides. Many families benefit from programs such as Medicaid and food stamps to make it through difficult times until they find sufficient employment. Critics of entitlement programs cite generations of families whose job is to stay on welfare for life. In working with wealthy families, I have seen they experience the exact same issues with entitlements. In those circles, entitlements generally refer to trusts. On one hand, trusts are a huge advantage to beneficiaries and can be the foundation for a lifetime of success in whatever venture they choose for themselves. And those same entitlements can also be used to disable an entire generation. It is clear from these examples that it isn't the entitlement but the mindset of the individuals utilizing them.

Industry Expert Insight

> In an interview with award winning financial trauma thought leader Rahkim Sabree, AFC, Sabree speaks about the historical precedent of Black families to distrust financial institutions, keeping those families from participating in the stock market or other investments. Sabree does see a cultural shift away from this pattern of distrust and avoidance due to increased minority representation in the field of finance. Sabree notes unhelpful patterns of thinking resulting from generational trauma including encouraging children to limit their expectations of success. Sabree also addresses the challenges of moving away from dependence on government systems for survival versus "pulling yourself up by your bootstraps" by presenting a more balanced view. Entitlements can be both extremely helpful to families and also demotivating. What matters is the mindset of the family system.

Now that we recognize our individual and collective stories are the unconscious drivers for our financial lives, let's journey on to Chapter Four, which is all about excavating and evaluating those stories.

Chapter Three Worksheet
What should young people do with their lives today? Many things, obviously. But the most daring thing is to create stable communities in which the terrible disease of loneliness can be cured. – Kurt Vonnegut

Disconnection from community, isolation, loneliness: these issues have only increased in the U.S. post COVID and the consequences are dire. Physically it results in premature death.[57] Economic downturns perpetuate loneliness, especially in older adults.[58] One purpose of the community is to provide a buffer for financial instability. When communities suffer an economic crisis, it is important to find ways to rebuild.

This chapter emphasized that **your community of origin** has unique ways of responding to tragedy. The health, fulfillment, and well-being of your community are critical to maintaining a thriving environment for you and your family. Therefore, we must look at how the community heals. Let's explore some questions about your community of origin.

Note for this exercise you can define a community any way you like - location of origin, religious community, etc.

Your Community of Origin Exploration
What memories do you have of your community coming together?

How would you describe your community's values?

What role do you play within your community? Is that role clear?

What myths and legends do you recall?

Note any struggles your community went through before you were born.

Do you have a way to honor those historical moments?

Who were the community heroes? Villains?

What are you most proud of regarding your community?

What is something you would like to change?

What are some community stories about money you remember being told?

What is your earliest understanding of your community's economic status?

What was the main industry?

How did your community respond when a family suffered a loss or financial tragedy?

Were there obvious signs of chaos due to finances in your community when you were growing up?

What did you learn from your community about money?

List the events in your community history that may have impacted your views on money.

Write down any significant insight you had from reading the chapter and answering the questions above.

Chapter Four: Building Blocks of the Money Story

Thus far, I hope it is clear the undeniable impact inherited trauma has on individuals, families and communities. All facets of our life, from the physical to the relational, can be touched by unresolved emotional pain. We also covered the important idea that all three systems (individual, family, community) are made up of energy bodies holding stories. And some stories are not particularly helpful.

In this chapter, we shift our focus from where the pain is stored (in the body) to *what* those bodies hold–stories. In explaining to my editor that our energy bodies hold stories, she asked, "Well, then what does inherited trauma sound like? How do we hear it in the stories people tell?"

Her questions were the reason for writing this book. My response at the time: "Unfortunately it often sounds like silence, Diane. Silence and denial."

Industry Expert Insight

> In her book, *The Curse of Inheritance*, succession expert Cindy Arledge explains that *"avoiders" leave their families lost* with regard to legacy. Cindy explains that a family's real issue is not the "avoidance of money but the avoidance of death" and its impact on descendants.

Buried by shame, many stories result in silence and denial. Avoiding hard conversations builds the barrier between you and your ability to thrive. Thus, the need to excavate those stories as individuals, families, and communities. From my experience, there is only one way to do this: Listen to ourselves, families, and communities like we've never listened before. Deep listening. And I do mean deep. We need to listen to our body's signals, to the words and tone of voice we choose and the stories we tell ourselves. We also need to listen deeply to others, requiring something hard to find these days: an uninterrupted presence in conversations. The power of one present conversation can completely change a life. It requires a practiced ear and a willingness to begin rewriting narratives to see a shift in our lives. In this chapter, we explore how we can listen for the root causes behind our dysfunctions, specifically related to wealth. Our journey begins with information I consider the most avoided and most difficult to uncover: the information *before* language, the pre-verbal experience.

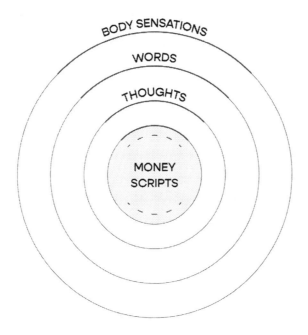

The Pre-Verbal Experience

From day one, our brains begin to make meaning out of the world. The one thing to consider is how exactly it comprehends at different stages of development. The *how* begins by understanding how memories are formed. Let's start by exploring the womb to age three memory building process. In general, our brain holds long term memories in two ways, implicitly and explicitly. Implicit is unconscious, automatic memory, such as riding a bike. Implicit memory recall also includes remembering how we feel (which actually begins in utero). Explicit refers to things we can consciously recall such as what we ate for breakfast this morning. In our pre-verbal phase (babies 0-3 years old) we only remember implicitly. As adults we do possess a vast implicit (unconscious) memory bank from that time.[3] Baby's emotional brains, the limbic system, are being heavily encoded with how the adults around them make them feel emotionally. A mix of emotions and body sensations stored in the body and brain incorporate the infant experience. At this point, the infant relies on emotions and sensations because the brain has yet to develop its language processing and storage facilities. As mentioned in Chapter Two, the first three years of childhood set the stage for our emotional and relational narratives. These are our stories of attachment to people, places and things (including resources like money) in the world around us and they begin to develop long before speech.

As adults, we tend to rely more on explicit memories throughout our day to day. However, we still possess a limbic system and live in the same bodies we had as infants. Therefore, we can't rely on literal memories alone to provide us with a full picture. We need to listen to body sensations, hunches, and feelings as well.

It is important to understand the infant and pre-verbal experience when we talk about money because:

1. This is the time when the attachment styles we discussed in Chapter Two develop.
2. It brings our attention to other types of information we may otherwise ignore, such as gut feelings, hunches, and intuitions.
3. It encourages us to prioritize child-rearing in the early years, knowing this impacts all areas of our child's life as an adult.

Formal practices that can unlock this pre-verbal world for adults include hypnosis, dream exploration, psychotherapy, and creative arts; essentially anything related to play. These tools can be used to link valuable information from the early years to the explicit memories shaping our decision-making. An alternative to the more formal ways of exploring is simply spending time in play both as a family team and individually. When families engage in play together they strengthen their bonds, thus making good teams without the need of formal interventions like therapy. However, there are other times when the bonds have experienced disruption where professional facilitation can help.

Having explored the importance of nonverbal data, let us turn our attention to the beginning of verbal communication–words.

Words
As we learned in the last section, we are hardwired to create order and meaning out of our experiences prior to understanding language. Beginning with our birth language, we begin to shape the world around us through our senses. As our brains develop, we start to place meaning on sounds and symbols, linking them into what we refer to as cognition. Those initial sounds and symbols are words. The modern-day linguist and poet, Laural Airica, explains the impact of our words on future generations when she states the following:

There is what I call an electro poetic force that causes words to migrate across centuries, cultures and countries to come into the same vibration so that you have words that do not share a history but they share a sound.... Words are magnetic. We are passing them like coins. We are passing them like currency.[23]

Airica explains that words pass on powerful subconscious meanings just by the way they sound. One example she shares are the words pray and prey. Words like these are homonyms: words that sound exactly the same in English, but with drastically different meanings. She suggests that when you hear a homonym like the word "pray," you cannot help but also associate it with "prey," albeit unconsciously. Airica encourages audiences to begin to pay very close attention to language and in doing so, harness the direction of their lives.

Because I work with adults in my practice, therapy generally begins with helping clients explore their circumstances using words. One of the extremely powerful and effective skills I frequently teach is the "reframe". A "reframe" helps us shift from one state to the next, sometimes by only changing one word in our thought pattern. A reframe I recently used in a client session involved a discussion around his description of himself as a "worrier" when it came to addressing the challenges in his family business. I suggested every time he sees himself as a "worrier" that he adjusts slightly to see himself as a "warrior" and champion for the family brand. We spent some time imagining how it would feel in his body to make this slight shift in thinking. The similarity in how the two words sound can aid in remembering our reframe practice. Another way to improve reframe practice is to do a check in with how the body feels when using the original word versus the new one. How might that shift in perception feel in your body during stressful times?

We have an individual responsibility to watch our words carefully. Not just for ourselves but for future generations. Our words can either build up or tear down.

What are some common words you use to refer to your family relationships and discussions around money?

> It's not just Airica who understands the power of words. Spiritual traditions have long held the belief that language is the key to creating our lives. The base language of Hindi, Sanskrit, is said to be made up of 16 vowels referred to as the "divine mothers." These 16 root sounds are said to direct and shape the material world.[59] These sounds parallel the first line of the Jewish and Christian Bible in which God literally spoke the cosmos into existence.[24] These spiritual traditions assert that to harness the tongue is to harness the direction of one's life. In our case we are going to harness our words in order to impact the direction of our financial lives and those of our children's children.

Thoughts

The "thought realm" or the logical mind is the place we adults spend most of our time. Unlike children, most of us spend very little time on creativity and play. Instead, daily activities revolve around planning, organizing, and executing ideas either alone or in conversation with others. For the most part, we are consciously removed from the influence of things like body sensations connected to words and double meanings of homonyms (words sounding the same with double meanings).

Because I work mostly with adults, the "thought realm" is usually the easiest place for us to start. I also begin here as a single thought carries more complexity than we sometimes give it credit. One thought links to a chain of other current thoughts as well as a chain of what I call "familiar feelings," which help us interpret the world. While in our "logical mind" most of the time, thoughts, much like our fascia, cannot be separated from the other ways we experience the world. The process of exploring thoughts is how to untangle them from all other unconscious information we might be blind to. One way to start exploring thoughts is to take an event, thought, emotion, or body sensation and make a chart like the one below. This is a classic activity from Cognitive Behavioral Therapy and I continue to find it very effective in teaching clients how to sort through thoughts, emotions, and body sensations as well as delving into the "why?" behind their actions. Here is an example:

LIFE EXPERIENCE
I find out I'm inheriting $20 million dollars from my grandfather who just passed away.

THOUGHTS	EMOTIONS	BODY SENSATIONS
This is fantastic. Now I never have to work again.	Excitement	Racing heart
I don't even know how to manage what I have.	Fear	Panic
But my friends still have to struggle.	Guilt	Heaviness in chest
What if people resent me or start to hate me for this?	More fear, despair	Increased heaviness in chest
It's ok though I am going to figure this out. I wonder who I need to get to help me with this news?	Confident, comfort	Reduced heartbeat, deep breath

ACTIONS
Go on online to try to find a financial advisor who understands me.

What do you notice about the chain of thoughts on this chart? Can you see how small shifts make a dramatic difference in the emotions and behaviors? This is only a snapshot of one thought pattern. The brain constantly forms many of these at the same time. Thoughts, linked to emotions and body sensations, make up what we will explore next, money scripts.

What's the Script/Scrip?

Defining your money script

The term "money scripts" was coined by Brad Klontz.[19] According to Klontz these money scripts are

- Learned in childhood
- Often unconscious

- Passed down through generations
- Just partial truths
- Responsible for financial outcomes[20]

Klontz explains these mostly unconscious, early established beliefs drive our financial behaviors, and are very strong indicators of income level and financial behaviors. Wealthy individuals indoctrinate different money scripts than lower and middle-class individuals. Klontz identifies four primary money scripts, the first three of which are detrimental to finances.

1. Money Avoidance
2. Money Worship
3. Money Status
4. Money Vigilance

You can take Brad's quiz and learn more about his work in healing financial trauma here: https://www.bradklontz.com/moneyscriptstest[21]

As you will see in the following, I remember internalizing specific messages about money as a child: work must be hard, money must be earned through grueling circumstances, and I shouldn't expect too much. By Klontz's assessment, I turned this messaging into what he calls "money vigilance." This money script is characterized by anxiety over money, an aversion to buying on credit, and a belief that money should be saved. Let's take a look.

Case Example: My Money Script
As I mentioned in Chapter Three, I grew up in a coal town not far from Little New York. Like many of these remote communities, mine was originally located far from banking institutions. Coal companies set up their own form of currency known as *scrip*. Scrip could only be used at the local company store. Working for coal companies that paid in scrip became a modern form of serfdom. With limited options for employment, employees developed a fierce loyalty to the company, as well as a sense of trauma bonding with peers created by working in deadly environments together.

My Sicilian immigrant grandfather, a coal miner, received wages in scrip. As a young girl, I interpreted his experience of being paid not in cash but in company tokens as a story similar to the feudal lords I learned about at school, who kept farmhands trapped in a life that would never extend beyond the castle walls. Well-rounded and curious, my grandfather loved learning, braved immigration, taught himself English, and became a skilled farmer and dedicated father. Yet, my 12-year-old-self reduced him to little more than a worker bee. I remember carrying sadness and pity for this man I never knew. I also carried guilt at the thought of him working very hard under life threatening conditions so that I could experience a better life.

As a trauma therapist, the word *scrip* has a unique and dual meaning and is a near homonym as discussed above. Scrip limited coal families' financial lives to the coal camp they worked for. Similarly, our family *scripts* can keep us stuck in the mental

CHILDHOOD

THOUGHTS	EMOTIONS	BODY SENSANTIONS	BEHAVIOURS
• Granddad was treated unfairly.	• Sadness	• Tight throat	• No noticeable outside behaviors.
• He was kind of like a slave.	• Grief/Sadness/	• Watery eyes	• "I can't control it so I will distract myself with play."
• He was separated from his mother and working really hard.	• Shame	• Confusion (feeling like I don't know which direction to go)	
• Making money means you have to leave your family and be sad.	• Sadness/Fear/Panic	• Heaviness in chest	
	• Fear/Grief		

ADULT

THOUGHTS	EMOTIONS	BODY SENSANTIONS	BEHAVIOURS
• I'm glad I don't have to work like granddad.	• Relief/Guilt	• Ability to breathe deeply mixed with Racing thoughts about how to resolve guilt.	• Intrinsic drive to work excessively.
			• I will work as hard as I can and save as much as possible.
			• "I must do anything possible to secure financial freedom and avoid working for someone else."

models we were born into.

Like me, you most likely established your internalized family narratives early in life. Your young mind processed the data through its unique lens, personal history, and spatial awareness. And today, it dramatically impacts your financial decision-making. How, you ask? Family Constellations Theory can explain.

As children we take these stories and develop what Family Constellations Therapy describes as "unconscious contracts." Unconscious contracts are agreements made with ourselves or others keep us feeling stuck, small, and constrained.[77] For example, returning to my grandfather, one of the clear takeaways my younger self believed was that earning money must be very hard, possibly even scary. Yet another layer in the story contributing to my ideas about money was the message that money is meant to take care of family and convey social status. When you read my story did you pick up on different messages or have a different understanding of the story's meaning? A person with different unconscious contracts from mine or a different money script may interpret my childhood experience completely differently (my sister certainly did).

Not surprisingly, Klontz's second point about money–that scripts are often unconscious–is where I devote most of my energy with families. I help dig up the buried stories relevant to the current generation. When we make the unconscious conscious in our lives, our family dynamics, and our community, magic happens. And we can only get there one way. We must understand our internal stories.

The Power of Personal and Family Scripts
To this point, all the above elements in the opening image of this chapter serve as the building blocks we use to construct stories. In order to create meaning, sensations are decoded through words, words link to thoughts, and thoughts link together to tell a story. For the purpose of this book, we will refer to the narrative therapy definition of story. According to narrative therapy, "story" is defined as:

- events
- linked in sequence
- across time
- according to a plot[22]

For example, loneliness and isolation often are dominant narratives of family leaders who earned fortunes far surpassing their parents and extended family. These dominant narratives are accompanied by conflicting feelings of guilt for not being able to "be normal" or relate to those around them, mixed with the desire to openly be proud of their accomplishments without fear of resentment from others.[22]

Dominant narratives not only affect the immediate behaviors of those experiencing them but can also inadvertently impact the behaviors of future decisions as well as the decisions of future generations. For example, if a parent feels shunned and resented by their family due to a sudden increase in wealth, a child may inadvertently internalize the narrative that if one has money, the family automatically isolates from them.

To add to the complexity, narrative therapy acknowledges our lives are "multi-storied" in the way that Arica describes. Due to various factions of our personalities, differing parts can interpret the same events through conflicting lenses. As time passes, lived experiences form those ever-changing, shape shifting ideas we call memories. Results of research studies prove time and again that memory is tricky. According to research at Northwestern University: "Every time you remember an event from the past, your brain networks change in ways that can alter the later recall of the event. Thus, the next time you remember it, you might recall not the original event but what you remembered the previous time.[25]

According to Donna Bridge "Your memory of an event can grow less precise even to the point of being totally false with each retrieval".[26]

The above tangled web of storytelling isn't just within the mind of one family member. When we look at the complexity of family stories from the perspective of family therapy, we begin to understand why so many challenges arise in family business meetings, estate planning and other important aspects of legacy planning. In families with inherited trauma, the boundaries are already blurred, and loyalty and trust are already strained. It is why clarifying these stories and collectively rewriting them proves so powerful.

How do we piece together the narrative? It begins with data. Like any good writer, we must start with a bit of research. The first and easiest place I find to start with clients is their own recollection of family stories. Note, due to a number of forms of family separation, some of us have little to no family stories. Never fear! There are other ways to access information about inherited trauma Including things like genealogy research and somatic body work. And those can be explored in another text. However, the majority of us maintain a collection of snippets from our family tree. For the purposes of healing, those are like gold.

Since these experiences occurred in early childhood (or are inherited through memories) I like to walk clients through an exercise I call "Core Memory Exploration." Let's take a look at an example in the next section.

Case Study: Core Memory Exploration

Jim and Sandra came to therapy wanting to improve communication and reduce cycles of communication chaos in the marriage. They described the need to stop arguments from escalating. They attributed the chaos to the stress of working and raising their four-year-old daughter. Shortly after beginning therapy, it became apparent the couple suffered from many unspoken money resentments in their marriage.

During consultation, I asked Sandra and Jim to write their earliest money memories.

- What discussions about money do they remember?
- Were there any sayings or phrases the family frequently used regarding money such as "money is tight"?
- Do you remember any general feelings about money and its purpose in the family?
- Do you have any memories of your parents' attitudes about spending?
- What were your parents' attitudes toward employment & their careers?
- Were there any money secrets or blatant traumas such as theft, legal issues surrounding money or the family business?

By exploring these questions independently, then as a couple, it became clear that while they experienced very different upbringings, their childhood money stories held overlapping themes. Sandra remembers feeling intense guilt from a young age due to her parents' choice to spend money on their daughter's childhood experiences rather than saving for the future. Her guilt continued into adulthood. Sandra also noted receiving mixed signals about money in her home because her father was a "saver" and her mother tended to "spend excessively" on anything her and her sister needed.

Jim experienced the opposite childhood but with a similar outcome. He remembers his mother, who grew up in extreme poverty, acting frugally, to the point of limiting food portions. On the other hand, his father, an immigrant, wanted to send money home to his family and invest in projects with his extended relatives. Conflict arose because Jim's mother disapproved of her husband sending money to the family in Asia.

Through this exploration, Jim and Sandra noted the overlap between conflicting messages about money, and the similar messaging around guilt associated with spending and extreme sacrifice due to the trauma of their parents growing up in poverty. By uncovering these core memories, Jim and Sandra understood their own patterns of money avoidance. They began to safely open up ongoing dialogue about spending and sticking to their family's financial plan without the need for guilt. Jim and Sandra did not initially come to therapy to discuss money. In fact, it took several months for the issue to even be identified as a major concern. It was a major "aha" moment when they realized how much resentment and unspoken pain they carried surrounding financial expectations and behaviors incongruent with their shared values. This was a great example of money avoidance.

As we see from Jim and Sandra's story, when we begin to explore core memories we often find overlaps between our pain points around money and the pain points of our chosen life partners. Remember those trauma bonds I spoke of? These trauma bonds exemplify the unconscious way unhealthy money patterns pass down through generations.

Chapter Four Worksheet

Words are sacred. If you get the right ones in the right order you can nudge the world a little. - Tom Stoppard

The purpose of this chapter was to emphasize that your **words hold extreme power**. I encourage you to be mindful of the words you speak and how they impact all aspects of your life, especially relationships. Use your words to lift up your family, community and yourself on a daily basis. Let's explore some questions about the language you use in your relationships including your relationship with money.

Language Exploration
Take a quick moment and write out some of your initial thoughts about family and wealth.

Without judgment, what are your initial associations?

Is there anything interesting about the words or phrases you've chosen?

Could these phrases have alternative meanings?

Have there been words or phrases your family used that hurt you? If so, what were they and why?

What were the words your family used to lift each other up?

Is there anything you notice about the supportive way your family communicates/d?

Might there even be echoes of pain in the support?

Write down any significant insight you had from reading the chapter and answering the questions above.

Part Two

Uncovering Inherited Trauma

Echoes of Inherited Pain

> In Greek mythology the mountain nymph, Echo, is an incredible storyteller. Zeus tasked her to weave a lying tale for his wife Hera to cover up his infidelity. Hera caught on to the deception and cursed Echo, taking away her storytelling abilities. Instead, Echo could only repeat the last word anyone said. Because of this, she could no longer connect with others and her spirit became heavy. One day, she fell in love with the stunningly handsome river god, Narcissus. A proud young man who only cared for himself, he lacked the desire or ability to connect with others and rejected Echo. She pursued him relentlessly, only ever able to echo the last word Narcissus spoke. Heartbroken and hopeless, she isolated herself in a cave and perished. Like Echo, we too are innate storytellers with the power to transform lives. In the same way that Hera could not (or was not willing) to be upfront and communicate her hurt with Zeus, inherited trauma removes our ability to articulate ourselves in a compassionate, honest way, leaving us to echo the suffering and behaviors of our ancestors throughout time.

In Part I, we defined how inherited trauma echoes through the experiences of individuals, families and communities. I hope it became clear from Part I that inherited trauma damages our self-esteem, relationships, and decision-making. Part I also demonstrates the shame and guilt associated with inherited trauma, which causes blind spots in our self-awareness. Through patterns of conscious and unconscious denial, we often sabotage our growth.

This section discusses what I know to be the hardest part for most individuals and families: Initially delving into relationships with themselves, their families, and their wealth. Let's begin with an assessment tool and some context for why I developed it. As we progress through the next chapters, we will review each pain echo (category) through the following:

- Specific examples of what these pain echoes may sound like internally or in conversation.
- We will then look at a story about what an individual, family, or community system may be thinking and expressing through their behaviors.
- The chapters in Part II will offer descriptions of the pain and possible mental manifestations of that pain. For example, a pain echo of insecurity may manifest as an anxiety disorder.
- Lastly, we will wrap up each chapter with a brief discussion of techniques that I find useful in addressing that specific pain.

Chapter Five: Accounting for Our Relationships

Succession is a point where people begin talking about the past. Because of this, families should go to therapy before succession planning. - Octavian Pilati, Writer and Speaker

Early in my career I held a Clinical Director position in community mental health programs throughout New York City. Outside auditing bodies intensely monitor these programs because they receive government funding. Our day-to-day operations revolved heavily on monitoring our own actions (albeit sometimes to the point of paranoia). However, I really appreciated the practice of self-assessment with this position. Self-monitoring habits, behaviors, and interactions, when done in a supportive, structured way, can produce success in a number of areas in our lives, including the management of our family legacies.

The opposite of thoughtful self-assessment is neglect. Inherited trauma encourages a certain level of neglect in individuals, families, and communities, which leads to blind spots. James Hughes Jr. notes that one major blind spot for individuals, family businesses, and family offices is the taking care of what he calls the Family Balance Sheet and Family Income Statement.[35] This balance sheet refers to the care of your family members responsible for protecting and generating income for the family. In the following sections we will explore the power of a family audit to revolutionize the way you care for your family's most precious assets: the individuals.

accounting:
An examination, reckoning and balancing of accounts so as to arrive at the true state of any transaction.

Why Family Audits?
Audits give us permission to slow down
I am consistently amazed at the mind's ability to tend toward rushing. For most working professionals and parents, not only are we caught up in the speed of life, but also the hurried way in which we approach the world. This hurried mode usually consists of quick decisions without much conscious input from the body. It presents itself as purely rational. In their book, *Slowing Down to the Speed of Life*, Richard Carlson and Joseph Bailey describe this mode as the processing mode. This mode is in charge of memory retention, data analytics, planning, and calculation. I refer to this as adult mode. As adults, most of us spend the majority of our days viewing the world through processing/adult mode. In doing so, we miss valuable insights and opportunities, such as access to deeper connections with family and creative ideas for our businesses. However, there is a second, free-flowing and underutilized mode, responsible for

spontaneous responses and creativity. I refer to this mode as child mode. This mode proves to be more beneficial in dealing with the unknown.[27] Slowing down, especially as a family, allows us to access our more neglected and often disregarded child mode.

When factoring generational hurts into an assessment of relationships and behaviors, we step into the unknown. Therefore, we need to utilize both minds. Reasoning and logic are tremendously important. But child mode expresses an insightful intelligence while attempting to heal painful family patterns. With both modes engaged, we tap into the wisdom of our whole selves.

Industry Expert Insight

> Slowing down conversations helps us uncover hidden fears and improve financial decision-making. Founder of North Financial Advisors, Cady North says Issues of shame, guilt and fear come up when we take the time to slow down our money conversations. Statements like "I am somebody who makes really good money. Thus far all I've done is put it in a checking account." They come to Cady afraid to admit they don't know how to make sound investments, that they have money and don't know what to do with it." By slowing down the conversation they can realize a plan is available and there is nothing to be ashamed about.

Audits help us respect ourselves, our ancestors, and our descendants

respect:

1. To feel or show deferential regard for; esteem or admiration.
2. To avoid interfering with or intruding upon.
3. To avoid violating.

Some clients come to me to address a single issue within the family unit. However, the physical or mental health of a particular family member can uncover larger issues in the family, including a major disruption in educational goals, business succession, or legacy planning. Family audits unlock narratives and assess how the narratives impact the family systems, including the ability to function as a team. Successful audits take into account the many facets of each individual member and how that member contributes to the family as a whole.

Case Example: Overcoming Family Curses
I first met with Jarek at the request of a nutritionist who thought Jarek might benefit from hypnosis to relieve digestive issues. Jarek stated he struggled with a fear of having a bathroom issue in public. Embarrassed, Jarek continuously missed out on social

opportunities and failed to hold on to good things in his life. My clinical intuition guided me to immediately ask about his birth story. From that question came an onslaught of information about the inheritance of digestive issues: It was a running joke amongst the family that the family was cursed. This curse extended into his ability to take care of himself financially, always feeling as if he couldn't "hold on" to money no matter how hard he tried.

With one question and a deep intention to really slow down, the story his body held—the pain of generations—came through. Unlocking that story, he began building a new type of freedom, a freedom where the family narrative shifted from shame and embarrassment to respect. Finally, he addressed not only his physical health issues but the psychological barriers contributing to unstable finances.

Audits define risks and inform plans to avoid future issues. They help establish rules of engagement for each member of the family. This can look like house rules, family business policies and procedures, and the beginnings of formal agreements, such as trusts and prenuptials. They take into account the many facets of each individual member and how that member contributes to the family as a whole. What if a family policy included addressing the issues behind the inherently harmful running jokes in our family? Or imagine the impact of Jarek returning to his family gatherings and shifting the narrative away from a family curse? Over and over again, I see the ripple effect of one person's healing permeating the family unit.

Audits Help Us Uncover Blind Spots
Family audits generally consist of interviews and qualitative tests to assess liabilities in the family system. They are a comprehensive review of a family's assets and liabilities. The purpose of an audit is to help families not only begin to develop a plan for known issues but to highlight strengths in order to enhance and build upon them. Most importantly, they help uncover blind spots.

Case Example: From Mental Illness to Thriving Young Adult
One of my greatest personal achievements involved working with a family over four years to rehabilitate their adult child who was experiencing severe mental illness. The young adult experienced a mental health crisis due to sudden wealth syndrome resulting in difficulty with daily living and an inability to achieve career goals and gain independence. I quickly realized the patient needed support growing in the following areas:

- A comprehensive mental health recovery plan
- Skills training for daily living

- Financial stewardship and education

I also found that the parents needed support in understanding the steps necessary to ensure their adult child reached a level of health and autonomy to thrive. With my training as a social worker, I helped develop a realistic plan of action and explained a realistic timeline to help their adult child meet their health, educational, and financial goals.

The reality is, sometimes we just don't know what we don't know. This family had so many things working in their favor. They were incredibly caring, concerned, and motivated. They also possessed the willingness to find the resources to help fill in the gaps. They just needed a little support uncovering blind spots.

Assessing for Liabilities
It is now your turn to perform a bit of auditing. The first step in the auditing process is an assessment. In this chapter, I will share the brief assessment I use with financial therapy clients. This assessment is relevant to anyone wanting to improve their relationship with family and money.

The process of auditing begins with understanding which liabilities have been passed down in our families.

The liabilities of inherited trauma can manifest as follows:

- Dissatisfied with our role in the family
- Abandoned
- Incompetent
- Unloved
- Outcast
- Out of control
- Angry
- Resentful
- Disgusted
- Numb

They impact the health of our family through:

- Lack of family governance
- Neglect of thought for future generations
- Inability to navigate transitions, illness, addictions, or death
- Poor financial health such as tax, credit, or legal issues (even if wealth is pres-

ent)
- Lack of planning for global disasters such as inflation, investment security, or acts of war

Keep in mind the different ways these inherited traumas may manifest in the second and third generations. The behaviors serve as initial warning signs that some type of trauma might be present in the family system.

Once we've identified the liabilities present, we assess your narrative or your unique understanding of personal, family and community history, which hold the keys to any dysfunctions you harbor surrounding family and money.

Before outlining the assessment, it is important to note that while the assessment describes common patterns and issues that are often labeled as mental health diagnoses in family members, <u>this assessment IS NOT a diagnosis tool for mental health issues</u>. Rather it is one I use to begin exploration of possible inherited patterns. It is strictly used in order to dive a bit deeper into the roots of generational trauma and develop a plan of action unique to your family. While I recommend everyone in your family complete the assessment, it isn't necessary. Because small changes to a system can have a dramatic impact, it is tremendously beneficial just to start with you.
The assessment covers 5 categories:
- Securities
- Emotional Currency
- Understanding Options
- Social Capital
- Emotional Bankruptcy

The adjoining chapters provide examples of how these patterns manifest through language and sometimes diagnoses from the western healthcare system. Again, scoring in one category or another **IS NOT MEANT TO DIAGNOSE a mental health disorder** but rather is a tool to possibly follow up with a mental health professional, to seek coaching or mentorship support.

The categories furnish a way of identifying behaviors and narrowing down and diving deeper into liabilities. They attempt to find answers to long standing problems you and your family system struggled with for a long time.

Inherited trauma causes a recurring question in us, "What do I keep doing wrong?" It perpetuates an irrational feeling of shame and guilt when in actuality the only thing you might be doing is unknowingly carrying the pain of your ancestors. If so, it's time to assess and practice letting go.

ECHO Legacy Assessment
Check the ones that apply to you within the past two months

Security (Category A)
___ I rarely or never feel like there is enough time, money, resources, etc
___ My loved ones would say I tend to overwork
___ I need to improve my stress management
___ I have struggles unique to inheriting or growing up with wealth
___ I fear conflict around family, business & money
___ Shame and/or guilt are common feelings for me
___ I fear for the financial future of myself or those I care for (including children & parents)
___ I question my worth in family/social situations

Emotional Currency (Category B)
___ I would like more energy
___ At times I feel emotionally chaotic
___ I would like to learn ways to relax
___ I am angry more than I'd like
___ I struggle with chronic mental health issues
___ I would like more ease & flow in my day to day
___ My sleep needs to improve
___ I would like to improve my connection to nature

Understanding Options (Category C)
___ Some aspects of my life could be more organized
___ Following through with certain projects can be difficult
___ I have some challenges when it comes to managing money
___ I tend to avoid financial or estate planning conversations
___ I am currently in a life transition
___ I have a creative dream that is unfulfilled
___ Some aspects of my life feel scattered or left perpetually unfinished
___ I have some challenges with concentrating

Social Capital (Category D)
___ I have some relationships I would like to improve
___ I struggle with conflict in my relationships
___ I would like to be a better negotiator

___ I am both a professional and a caregiver
___ I feel taken advantage of
___ I often feel isolated
___ I often feel I have to solve problems alone
___ I would appreciate more compassion from those around me

If you said yes to most of Category A, head on over to Chapter Six on Securities. There we will be discussing the importance of cultivating security in yourself, your decisions, emotions, and relationships.

If you said yes to most of Category B, you are welcome to skip to the chapter on Emotional Currency. This chapter discusses allowing your emotions to work for you rather than against you.

If you said yes to most of Category C, Understanding Options is the place for you. In this chapter we explore decision-making, decisiveness, and focus.

If you chose most of Category D, the chapter titled Social Capital is where you will want to focus your energy. This chapter encourages cultivating strong relationships to protect and strengthen your family and finances.

And if you checked a mix of categories, you may choose to explore all the chapters to see what resonates. Alternatively, I included a discussion in Chapter Ten, which focuses on Emotional (or real) Bankruptcy. This section explains two possibilities which can occur when many of the above issues happen simultaneously. This is an extremely painful place to be and can result in issues such as chronic illness and addictions.

Chapter Six: Securities

The *Insecure* Pain Echo

We can't afford that.

There isn't enough.

I'm not enough.

Nobody ever helps us.

We will never get ahead.

My projects always fail.

If I can just work harder, everything will be ok.

I have no time for myself.

security:

1. The state of being free from danger or threat.
2. A thing deposited or pledged as a guarantee of the fulfillment of an undertaking or the repayment of a loan, to be forfeited in case of default.

If you reached this chapter, your assessment probably noted some struggles with feelings of security in various areas of your life. As discussed in Part I, we know inherited trauma can dramatically impact our sense of safety and security in the world. If our ancestors experienced unsafe circumstances, we can unconsciously act out patterns of irrational fear in areas of our life where we are actually safe regardless of whether or not those traumas relate directly to money. Primary needs like finances, food, shelter, and sex directly relate to safety, security, and pleasure. If our ancestors endured severe, unsafe conditions, we might unconsciously seek out ways to put ourselves in danger (physically, financially, or otherwise). This chapter focuses on reclaiming the sense of safety you and your children deserve. Let's begin by taking a look at a typical narrative around security.

Money is Not Your Friend: Internalized Shame in the Family Wealth System

Daniel's family traveled the world while his father, a self-made millionaire, worked as a diplomat. In an attempt to teach responsibility, Daniel's father insisted Daniel work from a young age. While instilling a work ethic proved extremely helpful, the messages Daniel's father proffered about money appeared counterproductive. His childhood was filled with messages of shame for growing up in a financially comfortable environment. Daniel internalized the shame and developed a core belief about money: - *Money is not your friend or support.* Instead, money is something not to be counted on just because you possess it and to be feared because it could abandon you at any moment. The story Daniel shared in therapy reflected a childhood of emotional abandonment and an internal world of shame around his innate privileges. Daniel's father openly shared his perspective as an effort to protect Daniel from the pain of financial loss (trauma). However, as an adult, Daniel suffered from physical pain, including chronic back pain and crippling anxiety.

I hear this story of destructive (yet well-meaning) family narratives over and over again. Like Daniel, often the second or third generation will experience an onset of severe anxiety, chronic illness or unexplained pain. Where physical and emotional pain exist, there is often shame. In my experience, the best way to release shame is to become better observers of ourselves. Let's learn how in the next section.

Addressing Shame is the Doorway to Healing

Brene Brown, author, lecturer and world-renowned researcher on shame and guilt, defines shame "as the intensely painful feeling or experience of believing that we are flawed and therefore unworthy of love and belonging—something we've experienced, done, or failed to do makes us unworthy of connection".[28] Shame, an extremely destructive emotion, attacks our primary sense of security, resulting in a spectrum of mental discomfort, from generalized anxiety to paranoia. Two commonly used frameworks for understanding human needs are Maslow's Hierarchy of Needs as well as eastern yogic philosophy. I believe these two frameworks complement each other well because Maslow focuses on the overall needs of a human in a particular order and yogic philosophy links the identified needs with our physical responses to attainment of the needs. Here, we explore some similarities and overlaps in these paradigms.

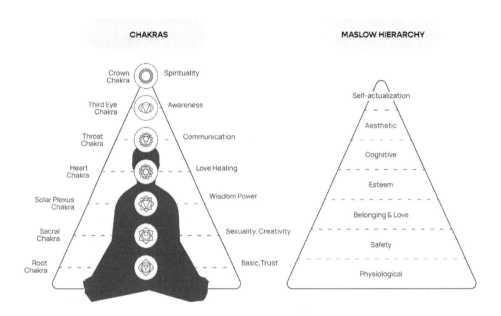

According to Maslow, the first two needs manifest as physiological (food, shelter, sleep, water, sex) and security (of food, family, health, employment). Because healthy finances form the basis for many needs in modern society, any financial traumas will overlap and impact these areas. If you examine Maslow's needs above, every need interacts with money in a different way. From money securing our base needs (food, water, shelter) all the way up to how we express our self-actualization (creativity, philanthropy, legacy), our relationship to money plays a crucial role.

While Western philosophy relies on Maslow, Eastern traditions lean to yogic philosophy. This system also provides a similar but slightly different framework for understanding primary human needs. The yoga sutras associate our financial needs, wants, and desires with the root chakra, which is found at the base of the spine in the pelvic/genital region. Yoga explains that this physical & energetic region stores the energy and emotions connected to our sense of security in all areas, from food, sleep, sex, and shelter to a sense of identity and the foundation for living our lives. The nerve connecting the center of this very sensitive area is referred to as the pudendal nerve. The name of this nerve comes from the Latin *pudendum*, meaning "parts to be ashamed of".[29] Its two primary functions are to control the muscles that enable us to go to the bathroom and to experience sensations such as sexual pleasure.

Recall the powerful nature of words and their meanings that we discussed in Chapter Four. Where is the logic in naming a body part "shameful"? Why is the energy center supporting our identity and need for security burdened with such a negative association? I reject the name of this nerve and find it completely appalling that anyone would assign a region of the body something to be ashamed of. That said, the shameful connotation surrounding this word resonates when we examine the emotional needs of trauma survivors who experienced an assault to this region of the body (such as sexual assault) or traumas associated with the emotional experiences of the root chakra (eating disorders, war, financial traumas). These traumas often result in tremendous shame. Shame rushes in and slams the door, trapping hurts inside the body, blocking our ability to access the words and memories needed to heal.

Cultivating the Observer-Self
Sometimes inherited trauma causes families to hold onto and act out patterns of severe criticism toward each other. The internalized shame associated with this behavior can be paralyzing. Shame creates warped versions of how we see ourselves. We feel embarrassed in public for no reason. Decision making may occur from a place other than confidence.

A great way to start uncovering the distortions caused by shame is to work on strengthening the "observer-self". What is the "observer-self"? From birth, we develop different "types of selves." The first to form, referred to as the emotional/child self, relies on our parents to regulate this "self," to keep us calm and safe. Parents accomplish regulation in many ways, including through nurturing and modeling. Until our brains develop more, parents serve other roles, such as serving as the logical decision-maker. They are also tasked with compassionately observing our behaviors in order to be effective parents. Essentially your parents' observer-self is modeled to us from birth. Unfortunately, our parents aren't perfect and they instill into the parent-child relationship their fair share of what I refer to as "thought viruses." Thought viruses serve as outdated or flat-out dysfunctional ways of thinking, which make our lives more difficult as children.

Because thought viruses exhibit contagious, sticky qualities, we assimilate them, carrying them into adulthood. As a mediator and psychotherapist, I see my primary role to be the compassionate observer for my clients as well as a teacher who can help them learn how to act as a compassionate observer of themselves.

The following image is what I use to describe our inner world to clients. I included "thought virus" in the model representing the ineffective behaviors we "pick up" from family or other caregivers, as well as through generational trauma:

Using Meditation to Unlock Hidden Shame
If shame dialogued, it would be saying obvious things like "You don't deserve to do that", "You don't deserve to feel safe", and "You're not capable". But one other major thought it certainly voices is "You don't need to look at me (shame) today". Shame lurks in the background, secretly pulling the strings of your life. It inherently closes us off from parts of ourselves that deserve a chance to be seen, have fun, make decisions and contribute. But one thing shame can't run from is stillness. And one way to find stillness is through meditation. It has personally and professionally served as a life-saving tool for me and many of my clients.

I have meditated for over 30 years. My first introduction to meditation occurred after stumbling upon *The Autobiography of a Yogi* and the *Sivananda Companion to Yoga* at our local library at 12 years old. The dedication to practicing stillness consistently from such a young age would not obviously prove itself so useful until I reached 33. March 3rd of 2014, I began experiencing seizures due to what we later learned resulted from Lyme disease. For years, I struggled with shocking neurological pain, burning sensations, muscle weakness, and fatigue. Old wounds from childhood also resurfaced, including a buried sense of intense shame. Because I cultivated the ability to step back from myself, to observe rather than get caught up, I retreated within, in a healthy way, to feel safe and secure no matter what occurred in my body. We all require a place inside ourselves to feel secure from the unpredictability of the outside world. Working to address and heal shame provides us that internal place. A Bible verse I learned as a child, Philippians 4:7, discusses the concept of "a peace that passes all understanding." I believe the process of meditation helps us cultivate that level of peace. The ability to enter into what I call "observer mode" provided me security in times of pain. It has also proved an invaluable skill in a profession where deep listening is key.

Case Example: Meditation to Cultivate the Observer Self
Not all meditations occur with eyes closed. Not all observation of self needs to be painful or boring. Observing the self first begins with awareness of what one needs.

This part we can't always perform on our own. We can employ people to help us step out of our own way. For some, the thought of being quiet and alone with our thoughts proves very difficult, to be avoided. I understand. If that's the case, I encourage you to start with making the body as comfortable as possible. If you must move then move. If you require stillness, stop moving. If that means being in nature, then step outside.

Let's take a look at a client example. James came to me struggling to focus on his business. He grew up in a middle-class family where his parents modeled patterns of overworking and feelings of never getting ahead. Despite James' ability to far surpass

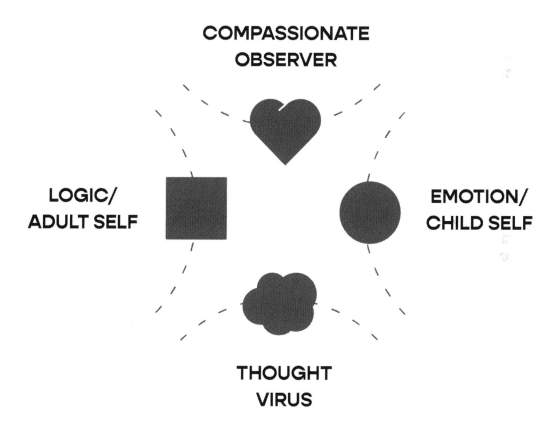

his parents' financial status and business success, he continued to carry the feeling of insecurity regarding "having enough." James also could not sit still. After a few sessions, it became evident James and I were not going to accomplish anything sitting and talking. At the time, I had an office around Wall Street and one day I asked James if he would like to take his session outside. James and I circled Zuccotti Park at a gentle pace, chatting about his business stresses and observing the tourist families, office workers, and pigeons out to lunch. James' entire demeanor changed while walking. His breathing became even. His face softened. I noticed his thinking appeared clearer.

While walking, we recognized the areas where he felt insecure taking steps forward in his business. Eventually, I had James breathe and walk while focusing on different areas of growth for his business, head tall, shoulders back, feeling the ground under his feet. James needed to walk, to meditate on the growth he wanted to see in his business. Walking enabled him to mentally sort through poor performing elements. He stepped into a more confident version of himself.

Parenting & Reparenting to Heal Shame
Like James, your only job as a child required you to feel out the world, learn everything you could, and be loved and cared for. That's it. And if your caregivers required anything more- for example, for you to raise siblings, be the emotional support of a mentally ill parent, or carry the blame for your parents' shortcomings- you may have been deprived of the time and attention you needed to learn your role as an invaluable innocent child, perfect in every way. You may have missed out on receiving messaging on your actual value. As you read this, you may recognize limitations your parents experienced. Or you may be completely cognizant that your parents failed to provide the support you deserved. This is where therapy creates a big impact. A large part of the work I do assists individuals in learning to reparent themselves. Reparenting "in self-help and some forms of counseling, [is] a therapeutic technique in which individuals are urged to provide for themselves the kind of parenting attitudes or actions their own parents failed to provide".[30] It is especially amazing when couples with young children come into therapy. The power of learning to internally "do-over" the emotional support your parents may have neglected has an enormous impact on the type of parent you become.

The book, *How to Do the Work* by Nicole LePera, describes four aspects to reparenting, all of which are essential for legacy creation:[31]

1. Emotional Regulation - Emotional regulation is "the ability to exert control over one's emotional state".[31] Without emotional regulation, we make decisions at the whims of our feelings.

   Morgan Housel, author of *The Psychology of Money*, talks extensively about the impact of childhood experiences on our relationship with money. He states these experiences are one of the most important factors in how we make financial decisions. Morgan also writes about how challenging it is to control emotions such as fear and greed and how those emotions prove extremely detrimental to sound financial decisions. Reparenting allows us to slow down and learn the skills to care for ourselves emotionally.[32] Learning emotional regulation helps us break free from irrational financial decisions that perpetuate feelings of shame.

2. Loving Discipline - Many people I work with are very successful, high achieving individuals who attribute part of their success to a very critical inner voice. This voice pushes them to do better than their peers and does not allow them to take breaks or fail. In some cases, listening to an inner critic results in tremendous success. I argue, however, it is not the most elegant way to achieve goals nor is it the most efficient. In fact, most high achieving individuals come into therapy when they feel they hit a wall in success. Often that wall is their inner critic. With regard to money, loving discipline looks like making financial management a priority, sticking to financial plans, and addressing addictions. Reparenting entails learning to motivate, encourage and achieve without the inner abuse.

3. Self-Care - Possibly the most overused term on the internet today, true self-care follows loving discipline. It is the ability to manage your day-to-day life in a way that nourishes you. Self-care examples include managing sleep, work stress, a healthy diet, and an exercise schedule.

4. Reclaiming a sense of wonder - Ideal childhood experiences involve curiosity, exploration, creation, joy, and play. Allowing yourself to truly enjoy life is the really fun part of reparenting. A key part of legacy creation incorporates this ability as it guides us to direct our time and financial resources to the activities we most enjoy.

Chapter Summary
This chapter has been an exploration in transforming money from an enemy into a friend. We explored ways to form more compassionate relationships with not just money but every single relationship in your life, beginning with the one you have with yourself. Practicing compassion begins with addressing feelings of shame. One strategy for transforming shame is to become a better "observer self", to slow down and watch what's happening rather than being reactive. Meditation is one strategy for cultivating the observer self. Then we explored the concept of reparenting. This is a great practice for both you and your ability to guide the next generation. Next, let's take another look at those pain echoes we identified at the chapter and identify some creative ways to reframe them.

Reframing Our Pain
If you recall from Chapter Five, one technique used to address the language of inherited trauma is the "reframe." For reframes to be effective they must 1) feel true, and 2) bring emotional relief. This section offers examples of reframes for the Insecure Pain Echo. Please remember if the revised statements do not meet these two criteria, adjust them until they do.

The *Insecure* Pain Echo with Reframes
We can't afford that. - If I really wanted to, I could purchase this. I choose not to spend my resources this way.

There isn't enough. - Although it seems resources are limited, I know I am resourceful and can find a way.

I'm not enough. - I am open to the idea that I am worthy.

Nobody ever helps us. - I am open to people helping me.

We will never get ahead. - Even though we are behind financially right now, we are taking steps to improve.

My projects always fail. - I've had failures and now I'm ready for a win.

If I can just work harder, everything will be ok. - I can focus for a moment on a time when things came easily to me.

I have no time for myself. - Where in this moment can I make time for myself?

Chapter Seven: Emotional Currency

The *Interrupted Emotional Flow* Pain Echo
I don't want to look at anything, especially my finances.

I wish this would all just go away.

It would be nice to have a different life.

I'll never get out of this mess.

F#% it. Let's go shopping.*

You only live once.

I'm so ashamed of what I've done.

How did I get here?

I give up.

Positive psychology takes you through the countryside of pleasure and gratification, up into the high country of strength and virtue, and finally to the peaks of lasting fulfillment, meaning and purpose. Seligman, 2002

If you reached this chapter, your assessment noted some struggles with lack of energy, motivation, or low mood around finances and other life issues. Part I explained how inherited trauma can cause us to shut down, hide, and possibly even abandon parts of our lives. If our ancestors experienced periods of deprivation or community poverty, we can unconsciously respond with a defeatist mentality. Issues of finances can seem overwhelming and just too much. This chapter focuses on the challenge of inherited trauma manifesting as emotional instability. In this instance I want to offer the strategic use of finding pleasure as a way to reclaim emotional stability toward finances and relationships.

Money is Out of My Control: Depression and Emotional Instability in the Family Wealth System

Money is referred to as currency for a reason. Like the energetic current running through our body, allowing our heart to beat, money and emotions serve as parallel streams, both representing our energetic health. The two require there in and out flow to be smooth and steady. They rely on a clear direction with clean, contained space to flow.

Unstable emotional states interrupt that flow and its direction. Experiences like depression cause our families and financial lives to live in cycles of despair. When feeling hopeless, we reach for short term fixes that often appear to be forms of attention seeking, even if negative. In the financial realm these short-term fixes can include avoidance of people and responsibilities and overspending. Rather than grasping at quick fixes, it's imperative to address the root of the problem, restoring emotional energy to its natural flow. It is important to learn how to properly move emotions through the body and use them as allies rather than weapons against us. Instead, we can turn our attention to ways we can find pleasure in the process of keeping and holding onto resources.

Pleasure as a Gateway to Resilience Building

Focusing on the pleasurable part of our day-to-day activities can have a profound impact on how we experience our lives. Turning toward pleasure encourages feelings of gratitude and turns our minds toward the wealth of opportunity our world offers for growth. When we grow up in thriving families and communities, it often feels easier to step into the excitement of financial growth. But it's the down turns in individual circumstances, family experiences of deals gone wrong and community disasters that really test our ability to maintain a positive mindset. Remember "Little New York" from Chapter Three? Let's revisit this scene and hone in on an example of someone who leaned into healthy pleasure seeking for his resilience.

At the height of Welch, WV'S prosperity, the town prided itself as one of the most ethnically diverse cities in the country. In the 1940's, the coal boom exploded Welch's small population to 6000. The community valued and respected diversity. According to Mark Myers, writer for the West Virginia encyclopedia, "McDowell County, which had no slave population and no free blacks after emancipation, became the state's center of African American population in the industrial era. McDowell County blacks established a power base within the state and local Republican Party, governing communities such as Keystone in the early twentieth century and regularly sending delegates to the state legislature".[60] It seemed the sky was the limit. And that attitude resonated through the generations. Even though McDowell County fostered in many ways an environment of diversity and resilience, the decades-long decline into poverty resulted in systemic financial traumas in its community members including high rates of incarceration, drug use and unemployment.

Despite community narratives and collective trauma, it is important to note individuals and families develop their own strategies for resiliently approaching financial devastation in their community. Such is the case with Ramon Stuart, President of West Virginia University Technical College. A Welch native, Stuart remembers possessing a strong work ethic and personal responsibility from a young age. He also remembers finding enjoyment in making and holding on to money. The son of a single mother who supported herself through a college degree, Stuart described stepping into a provider role at an early age. He spent his time outside of academics making money by running errands for all the widows in the community. As young as 11, Stuart had a newspaper delivery route and mowed lawns for money. Early on, he learned the importance of diversifying financial resources in order to thrive. Stuart explained that one of his teachers, Mr. Williams, gave him the foundation of what a man could and should be. "Mr. Williams, the father of nine children, built his home by hand "from the digging of the footer to the last shingle on the roof." When Stuart asked how he found time to be a teacher and build a home, Mr. Williams replied, "Who else was going to build it for me?" Mr. Stuart learned the unspoken narrative of self-reliance from his teacher: The attitude that anything was possible and the confidence to overcome all obstacles.

Additionally, Stuart shared he "doesn't ever remember the notion of having to work [as a child]." Stuart describes work as an example of what we might today refer to as "gamification." Gamification is simply the act of turning something which might be perceived as work, tedious or mundane into a game to increase enjoyment and motivation.⁸⁰ Resilient minds plan for the future while also finding pleasure in and making the most of the present. Stuart exhibits all of these qualities. When asked what he believes could have made the most difference in the Welch community over the last 50 years, Stuart explained that future planning would have made the difference. If the community had diversified its economy and prepared to pivot away from coal mining, the community may not have faced the economic decline it suffered. Stuart offers insights individuals, families, and communities can enact to safeguard from such fate.

The planning required to safeguard against financial devastation requires:
- An audit of our family and collective history
- A vision of where we want to go
- A clear plan for getting there
- Safeguards and measures for managing risk

This type of planning does not have to be boring or stuffy. In fact, the process of evaluating, organizing, and looking forward as a family is meant to be deeply rewarding and even fun. Speaking of fun, let's explore the benefits of positive psychology and flow states.

Positive Psychology and Flow States

Being in what positive psychologists refer to as a *flow state* is one of the most pleasurable states of mind we can experience. Flow states are defined by positive psychology as being completely and totally immersed in a task. This immersion includes feeling energized, fulfilled, and enjoying the process.[78] Essentially, flow states are the ultimate good time when being engaged in an activity. As a clinical hypnotherapist, I use hypnosis with clients regularly to help intentionally induce flow states for things like peak performance and overcoming fear of speaking. But hypnosis isn't the only way to induce a flow state. Research shows there are three other tools you can reach for to induce flow: practicing gratitude, mindfulness practices (just 11 minutes of meditation counts), and exercises (just 20 to 30 minutes per day).

We also know that practicing flow states can relieve depression. For example, research shows a 20-minute walk in the woods outperforms most antidepressants. In fact, it is important to note that the brain actually already possesses all the "feel good" chemicals it needs to pull itself out of a depression. Practicing flow states are a way to get those chemicals going without the needs of pharmaceuticals, recreational drugs, or alcohol.[88]

But what does this have to do with family, relationships, and money? If we discover ways to achieve flow states in our interactions with family and money, we have found a way to overcome any negative feelings of resistance toward taking care of the day to day such as showing up to work, family business meetings, and/or sitting down to evaluate finances. In fact, one of my favorite activities to help clients with is how to experience more pleasure in not just the mundane day to day but in the tasks they really dislike. Just as in the example of Dr. Stuart, one way to induce flow states in the day to day is by turning those tasks into a game.

Gamification as an Entry into Improved Emotional Flow

As mentioned earlier, gamification is the process of applying game elements to non-game tasks such as learning and work environments. The benefits of gamifying activities encourage us to step out of depressed states and experience its opposites - pleasure, enjoyment, and a sense of accomplishment. Gamification benefits include:

1. Increased engagement and motivation
2. Enhanced learning and skill development
3. Improved behavior chance and goal achievement
4. Collaboration and healthy competition[71]

Because we are focusing on using gamification not just for learning and development (actions most of us might feel emotionally neutral about), but for unpleasant situations (maybe even emotionally painful), I like to ask clients: What would it be like if this task was actually pleasurable, possibly even fun? In examples such as monthly fights between couples over finances or the fear of looking at personal finances, it may take a few conversations to increase motivation around pleasure even being possible in those situations. And that's OK! The main goal is to realize that you can feel pleasure and flow in ANY situation. It's just a matter of practice.

Chapter Summary
In this chapter we explored the unique challenge of uncontrollable or depressed emotional states impacting our ability to make sound decisions related to earning potential, spending, and communication about money. We then explored an example of what makes us individually resilient in the face of external stress. We identified one way to build resilience was to focus on developing flow states, specifically through the technique of gamification. Now that we have explored the concepts of pleasure and gamification for emotional wellbeing, let's move on to reframing our thoughts associated with waves of emotions.

Reframing Our Pain
If you recall from Chapter Five, one technique used to address the language of inherited trauma is the "reframe." For reframes to be effective they must 1) feel true, and 2) bring emotional relief. This section offers examples of reframes for the *Interrupted Emotional Flow* Pain Echo. Please remember if the revised statements do not meet these two criteria, we adjust them until they do.

The *Interrupted Emotional Flow* Pain Echo with reframes
I don't want to look at anything, especially my finances. - I am learning to confront my finances with ease and fun.

I wish this would all just go away. - I can call upon my ancestors to help me address these challenges.

It would be nice to have a different life. - I'm learning to appreciate and make the best of the life I have.

I'll never get out of this mess. - All things end and I am looking forward to this struggle leaving my life.

F#% it let's go shopping. - In this moment I can practice mindfully making a decision. I can also practice being satisfied with what I have.*

You only live once. - It's ok to pause before I make this decision. I can still have fun and consider the consequences.

I'm so ashamed of what I've done. - I am open to forgiving myself for my actions.
How did I get here? - I will find someone to help me review the decisions I made in order to prevent them going forward.

I give up. - Even though I feel like giving up, I'm going to keep going and find ways to make it feel good.

> Once you have answered **yes** to the question: *"Is it possible to make this situation more pleasurable?"*, we can then start to practice. Below are a few suggestions on finding pleasure in money related challenges:
> 1. Personal Finance: Add some healthy competition - against yourself. If you are looking for a little internal competition to encourage savings, apps like Acorn and SavingsQuest could help you save up to 25% more than you were before signing up.
> 2. Challenging money conversations: Try the *This Is A Test: Only A Test* exercise in your next conversation, if you find yourself wanting to avoid conversations with family related to money. My top suggestion for clients is to go into the next conversation more as an experiment and less tied to an outcome. You can choose to be more of an observer of the other person's behavior or possibly alter your communication approach in some way.
> 3. Work motivation and satisfaction: If you find yourself hating your current job, the challenge is to turn your attention to what is pleasurable in the moment. The only rule is, you can't say "nothing". Ask yourself:
> How can I make this day more pleasurable?
> How can I make this day more about me?
> Where is the pleasure here?

Chapter Eight: Understanding Options

The *Indecisive* Pain Echo
Why did I buy that?

I'll do it later.

I forgot to pay the bills.

It's impossible to plan for the future.

I'm so frustrated I can't make a decision.

I just don't know what to do anymore.

Maybe if we move we will get our life together.

Why can't I stick to anything?

It takes so long to accomplish anything.

option:
1. The act of choosing; choice.
2. The power or freedom to choose.
3. The right, usually obtained for a fee, to buy or sell an asset within a specified time at a set price.

If this chapter resonates with you, you or someone in your life might be struggling with what we mentioned in Chapter Five as the "adult or logical mind." Our adult/logical mind refers to the prefrontal cortex located in the frontal lobe just behind your forehead. For the most part, we remain unaware of the complexity required to perform tasks like bill paying and developing a basic budget. But for the brain to effectuate the chores, a number of processes need to work perfectly. For the prefrontal cortex to perform its job, the emotional regulation center of the brain also must be working optimally. This is where unresolved trauma becomes an issue. Trauma forces our emotional system into overdrive, requiring the downregulation of the prefrontal cortex, proving difficult to make decisions.[33]

My Money Life is A Mess: **Trauma/ADHD, Lack of Focus, and Family Wealth**
Jen came to me trapped in an abusive relationship. Engaged, she was seriously considering marriage despite knowing her toxic relationship. The main driver proved to be her fear and insecurity around the ability to manage her money. With her current partner, at least she felt financially stable. Jen lacked self-esteem at work, constantly worrying she would be let go despite earning excellent reviews from management. To make matters worse, she described herself as a "terrible money manager." She often spent money as a way to relieve stress, frequently paying bills late and relying on her fiancé to manage the day-to-day expenses. Jen grew up in a financially privileged but emotionally neglectful home. While she had everything she needed materially, she consistently received criticism, comparing her achievements to those of her older brother. Diagnosed with ADHD as a child, Jen took Adderall for years. Despite the diagnosis, extensive trauma processing in combination with ketamine infusions allowed Jen to find focus and end her dependence on Adderall permanently. Because of this a cascade occurred, confidence improved and she finally made the decision to leave the unhealthy relationship. Let's take a look at the complex way we, like Jen, make these major life decisions.

The ADHD/Trauma Overlap
Defining Executive Function
According to the University of California San Francisco Aging Center:

> The term *executive functions* refers to the higher-level cognitive skills you use

to control and coordinate your other cognitive abilities and behaviors. The term is a business metaphor, suggesting that your executive functions are akin to the chief executive monitoring all of the different departments in order for the company to move forward as efficiently and effectively as possible. The fundamental skills of executive function include proficiency in adaptable thinking, planning, self-monitoring, self-control, working memory, time management, and organization.[33]

Executive functioning challenges can include struggles with personal budgeting and finance, making it difficult to keep track of bill payments, taxes, and budgeting. There can be a number of reasons for these challenges ranging from lack of education to trauma.

Lack of Financial Education in Childhood
With regard to succession planning, I can cite numerous examples of first-generation leaders who neglected to teach their children basic financial management. They then approach their adult children, insisting they get up to speed with money management. Attempts at educating them include sending high-level articles and books on the subjects of investing and accounting. For the next generation inheritor with executive function issues and possibly low self-esteem related to money, these efforts completely shut the inheritor down. Adult children may define themselves as incompetent and avoid seeking the appropriate level of support to begin the learning process. In my work, the first order of business is to encourage an environment where the inheritor feels safe to ask questions. Therefore, a more realistic approach requires assessment of their needs of support concerning money management. Then, direct them to the resources appropriate for their needs. This can include tailored budgeting and personal finance classes as well as working with an executive functioning coach to develop personalized systems and tools.

ADHD & Executive Functioning
Attention Deficit Hyperactivity Disorder (ADHD) is probably the most commonly known executive function disorder. Research indicates the parts of the brain controlling executive function appear less developed in those with ADHD. This is also true in adults who experienced trauma as children. A 2019 research study demonstrated the connection between a mother's stress and the manifestation of ADHD in children.[36] Post-traumatic stress responses and ADHD share similar symptomology. Some of those include:

- Fidgety
- Difficulty focusing

- Hyperactivity
- "Acting out"
- Challenges with organization
- Challenges managing emotions

Additionally, ADHD and childhood trauma share other overlaps. For example, if a child possesses a genetic predisposition toward ADHD, a traumatic event may exacerbate symptoms. In Jen's case, it remained unclear whether she truly suffered from ADHD or lived with post-traumatic stress. Given her family history of emotional abuse and neglect, along with the shame of being deemed financially irresponsible, and the ongoing abuse from her fiancé, obviously Jen required treatment for trauma and not just Adderall.

It is important to note we can struggle with executive functioning without having ADHD or post-traumatic stress. Other factors impair executive function, such as chronic health conditions and the stress of major life transitions. For the well-being of individuals and family systems, it is important to address the needs of family members with executive function challenges like ADHD.

Industry Expert Insight

Here's a common scenario: We start a new behavior, and a week later, we fall off and beat ourselves up. "See? I'm not consistent with anything. So why bother?" I have countless systems and hacks to make my life easier and get more done. And I'm far from 100% consistent with any of them. And I'm okay with that. When I mess up, I just get back at it and try to diagnose why I fell off. No matter how inconsistent you are, stop berating yourself, give yourself some grace, and get back on the pony again. - Alan P Brown, ADD Coach.[94]

From ADHD to Post Traumatic Growth

Jen provides a perfect example of someone who overcame trauma, gaining tremendous growth and insight from the process. In fact, Jen transformed her ADHD diagnosis and PTSD into what we refer to as Post Traumatic Growth (PTG). PTG is defined as "positive psychological change experienced as a result of struggling with highly challenging, highly stressful life circumstances."[38] A hallmark of PTG includes the ability to reframe one's view of a situation. The outcome of those reframes leads to an increase in the following:

- Appreciation of life.
- Relationships with others.

- New possibilities in life.
- Personal strength.
- Spiritual change.[38]

PTG frees up emotional energy and allows the mind to make decisions with more rationality and discernment. If you experience executive function challenges related to inherited trauma, I hope we can unlock the pain and transform it into something useful.

Whether you have a formal ADHD diagnosis or you generally feel scattered, unable to finish projects or make decisions, there are actionable steps you can take to improve your overall executive function. Trauma processing is a great place to start. Beyond that there are many resources to address a diagnosis of ADHD such as working with an executive function coach.

The next section covers a list of ideas and resources to improve executive function.

Organization
1. Writing
I highly encourage all my clients to take notes during our meetings. This serves many functions, including accountability for progressing towards goals. But there are far more benefits. In fact, over 200 studies show the benefits of writing for emotional well-being and cognitive processing. Some examples of writing to improve executive functioning include list-making, storytelling through blogs or journals and reflective writing– the act of reflecting on work interactions to improve processes and outcomes.[55]

2. Chores as therapy
Many coaches and thought leaders advocate for paying for the day-to-day chores which can be described as time sucks, things that take us away from the act of earning money. But there might be an alternative way of thinking of these activities of daily living. What if we were actually outsourcing something tremendously valuable to our mental health? This is the thought process behind the concept of chores as therapy of which there is a tremendous amount of research.[81] Laundry for example, my husband hates it. To me, it is one moment during the week where I can step away from my phone and be present with the clothes that bring me joy. My tiny dogs often join in. They have made a habit of wrestling around while I listen to soft music, focus on folding my things into neat little piles, and giving my brain a break from the other more stressful things in my day.

3. Access nature
What if improving focus were as easy as spending time with trees? There is research

that having access to green spaces improves our ability to pay attention.[82] One fascinating bit of research shows that time spent in nature can enhance our ability to recall numbers or objects in reverse, referred to as the *backward digit-span task.*[83]

4. **Use your planner**

Simple but effective, the use of a daily, monthly, and yearly planner is incredibly helpful for mental health. Implementing systems into your daily routine including goal tracking can greatly reduce stress and improve quality of life by allowing you to see your progress. For a macro look at your year, I highly recommend end/beginning of year reviews for yourself and your family followed by the use of The 12 Week Year.com

Decision-Making

1. **Study** *The One Thing: The Surprisingly Simple Truth Behind Extraordinar Results (2012)* **by Gary Keller**

At one point or another most of us struggle with identifying and taking action on the next best steps for our family or business. Keller's book encourages readers to clearly define their purpose and values in order to drive decision-making. From there Keller critiques multitasking and instead argues that our only task is to focus on asking what Keller calls "The Focusing Question," which asks readers to consider one thing they can do in pursuit of any task or goal to make all else easier or unnecessary. Keller describes the process of improving the questions we ask ourselves in an attempt to make better decisions.

2. **Learn** mental models

A mental model is simply a framework of how something works. Mental models help us drive decision-making. They guide our perceptions and behavior. There is no single model that works for all scenarios. That's why it is helpful to have an understanding of different types of models for decision-making.[79] Game theory is one example of a mental model. It is the study of interdependent decision-making. One resource for learning more about Game Theory is: *The Art Of Game Theory: How To Win Life's Ultimate Payoffs Through The Craft Of Prediction, Influence, And Empathetic Strategy* by Wisdom University.

3. **Understand your cognitive biases**

Through therapy and coaching we can begin to uncover cognitive biases. A cognitive bias is a way of thinking that is opposed to rational judgment. Cognitive biases are the stories we make up about the world around us that are not based in reality. By being able to recognize our biases we can overcome them and make better decisions.

Chapter Summary
In this chapter we explored the strain trauma can put on the decision-making process by overburdening the emotional centers of the brain, lessening our ability to access its logic-processing functions. We learned that the ability for our mind to organize and act upon a plan is referred to as executive functions. We also explored the diagnosis of ADHD and how its symptoms can look similar (and sometimes overlap) with trauma responses, causing even more complications in goal accomplishment. We then examined the concept of post-traumatic growth and how it can free up the energy to get organized and accomplish more than we ever thought we could. Lastly, we looked at some tools and resources for improving executive function skills such as organization, focus, and decision-making.

Reframing Our Pain
If you recall from Chapter Five, one technique used to address the language of inherited trauma is the "reframe". For reframes to be effective they must 1) feel true, and 2) bring emotional relief. This section offers examples of reframes for the *Indecisive* Pain Echo. Please remember if the revised statements do not meet these two criteria, we adjust them until they do.

The *Indecisive* Pain Echo with Reframes
Why did I buy that? - Even though I feel guilty for this purchase, I have options. I can return it. If not, I can slow down and answer this question - Why exactly did I buy that?

I'll do it later. - I'm working on taking care of things as they come up.

I forgot to pay the bills. - I am capable of finding systems to help stay on top of bills.

It's impossible to plan for the future. - Even though it feels impossible to plan for the future, I can still do my best and look for small wins.

I'm so frustrated I can't make a decision. - There have been times when I made good decisions. I need to remember those.

I just don't know what to do anymore. - Even though I feel at a loss right now, I can call and speak to someone about my circumstances.

Maybe if we move, we will get our life together. - What can I do at this moment, given what I have, to make my circumstances better?

Why can't I stick to anything? - Let me review my accomplishments so far.

It takes so long to get anything accomplished. - Realistically, how far am I from finishing?

Chapter Nine: Social Capital

The *Broken Attachment* Pain Echo
I need attention to feel valuable.

Shopping is how I relieve stress.

If I were different people would like me better.

I can be impulsive with my spending.

I wish I could be confident about my decisions.

My boss hates me.

I'm not sure I know who I am.

My family ruined my life.

People say I'm unreliable.

Why should I have to show up for people, they don't show up for me?

social capital:
1. The goodwill, sympathy, and connections created by social interaction within and between social networks.
2. The value created by social relationships, with expected returns in the marketplace.

If this chapter resonates with you, you or someone in your life might be struggling with the ability to form and keep healthy, supportive relationships in at least one area of your life. And possibly this is your financial world. There may be struggles with maintaining employment, finding trusted advisors, or being able to have productive money conversations with family. And at the base of it all there may be a deep wound of feeling abandoned, unseen, or misunderstood. Money may even be used as a way to hold on to relationships. This chapter will explore the connection between attachment wounds, specifically abandonment and its impact on finances.

Money Can Buy Me Friends: Abandonment Wounds, Borderline Personality Disorder, and the Family Wealth System

Erin came to therapy with an established diagnosis of borderline personality disorder (BPD). According to the Mayo clinic:

People with borderline personality disorder have a strong fear of abandonment or being left alone. Even though they want to have loving and lasting relationships, the fear of being abandoned often leads to mood swings and anger. It also leads to impulsiveness and self-injury that may push others away.[84]

Erin specifically wanted to work on having more control over her finances. As Erin and I reviewed her thoughts, emotions, and behaviors associated with money, a clear link developed between her fear of abandonment and her spending habits. Most financial decisions preceded cautionary thoughts of the way she might be accepted through her clothing purchases. She also spent freely on her friends, paying for trips, and lavishing them with gifts. We discussed the behaviors that were not the issue. The underlying motivation for the behaviors resulted from a fear of being alone. The work from then on focused on how to build genuine stable and safe connections without the need for spending. Over time, Erin worked to rid herself of individuals using her for financial resources and replaced them with connections willing to help her based on reciprocity and genuine care.

Healing the Abandonment Wound

S.W.I.R.L is an acronym introduced by renowned abandonment therapy expert, Susan Anderson to explain what she describes as the five stages of abandonment. In this section, we will review the five stages and how to compassionately address each.

> **1. Shattered** - When we experience (or re-experience abandonment) it can initially be shocking, as if our world has been shattered. The shock phase, similar to experiencing a loss, this stage can be extremely painful and all-encompassing.
>
> **2. Withdrawal** - This stage describes the feelings of longing and wanting to be reconnected to the person, (object, or place) you were attached to. Similar to withdrawal from drugs, the opiate centers in the body create an intense physical sensation of craving.
>
> **3. Internalizing** - This is the stage in which we believe that, because we were rejected, there is something inherently wrong with us. Our self-esteem is damaged. We may self-criticize, feel isolated, and experience self-doubt.
>
> **4. Rage** - The fourth phase is our nervous system's attempt at fighting back against all the hurt we have experienced. Anger outbursts or self-abuse can occur.
>
> **5. Lifting** - As the rage subsides you begin to feel some relief after the release of energy. You begin to feel like you can engage in life again.[85]

This cycle can last hours, days, or years. It's never too late to begin addressing an abandonment wound, even if it has lasted many years. Below are two ways of healing through abandonment.

Individually - Some therapeutic styles to help with abandonment wounds include dialectical behavioral therapy (DBT) and trauma-focused therapies such as eye movement desensitization reprocessing (EMDR).

Family - Collectively, families can work on abandonment wounds. Together you can explore attachment-based family therapy.

The benefits of healing abandonment wounds extend far beyond self-esteem and family dynamics. They form the basis of a healthy relationship with everyone we interact with. And for the purposes of financial health, they are the foundation of growing our social capital.

Addressing Trauma Improves Access to Social Capital

The example of Erin at the beginning of the chapter demonstrates one way addressing trauma improves social resources. And when it comes to maintaining wealth, social resources mean so much. In fact, many social researchers linked higher economic growth rates, with one study showing a fivefold increase in household income based on the health of social networks.[61] Social capital is defined as "the networks of relationships among people who live and work in a particular society, enabling that society to function effectively".[37] Social capital includes social groups and institutions that share common values and goals. As with financial capital, when an individual or family possesses sufficient social capital, they gain access to resources to help them achieve their goals. The one difference between financial forms of capital and social capital lies in the fact that unlike financial capital, social capital is not depleted by use.[42] Families access social capital on an individual, group, and societal level. Examples of social capital include borrowing something from a neighbor (individual), a sorority sister connecting you with a potential job offer (group), and accessing public spaces (societal).[37]

In *Family Wealth: Keeping it in the Family – How Family Members and Their Advisors Preserve Human, Intellectual and Financial Assets for Generations,* James Hughes Jr. states healthy social capital is the outcome of successfully nurturing the members of one's family. Hughes writes: "...the amount of social capital a family has is a function of how well each family member knows himself or herself and how he or she expresses that knowledge in dealing with the larger world".[33] While I do agree, Hughes' book does not address the impact of dysfunctional relationship patterns within the family and the toll it takes on building social capital. As in the example of Erin at the beginning of the chapter, unhealthy relationships cause financial strain on the individual, family, and community. Hence the need to examine motivations for keeping or letting go of relationships. We scrutinize this through intentional inquiry.

Taking inventory of relationships manifests as one of the most important tasks any family performs, beginning within the family unit. Given the fact family conflict prevails as a primary reason for succession failure, it would be wise to begin healing these interactions. Family interactions form the basis for all our relationships in the larger society. Therefore, if they prove dysfunctional, it stands to reason they impact other relationships. We must evaluate and improve these first. The foundation of acquiring social capital is one's capacity to establish and maintain successful interpersonal relationships. This begins with your family but ultimately extends to all forms of social capital.

Industry Expert Insight

Robert Putnam's 2000 book Bowling Alone is still very relevant 25 years later. Putnam witness the beginning of the downfall of community engagement in the US and wrote the following:

Community connectedness is not just about warm fuzzy tales of civic triumph. In measurable and well-documented ways, social capital makes an enormous difference in our lives. . . [S]ocial capital makes us smarter, healthier, safer, richer, and better able to govern a just and stable democracy.[87]

The Three Types of Social Capital - Bonding, Bridging, and Linking

There are three types of social capital in social capital theory: bonding, bridging, and linking. As you read the descriptions of social capital in the next section, think about how you might see generational trauma impacting these areas. At the end of the chapter, I offer solutions for strengthening each area beginning with the family.

Bonding

Bonding capital takes place between groups who hold many things in common. They tend to live in the same geographic region and share similar values and norms. Bonding capital serves as the stepping stone to other types of capital. This group includes family members and close neighbors. Strengthening these relationships sets us up for success in the other two types.

Bridging

Research and Founder of the Institute for Social Capital, Tristan Claridge states: "Bonding social capital is good for 'getting by' and bridging is crucial for 'getting ahead'".[52] Bridging refers to relationships we foster with people outside our immediate social group. According to Claridge: "Bridging social capital allows different groups to share and exchange information, ideas, and innovation and builds consensus among the groups representing diverse interests. Overlapping networks may make accessible the resources and opportunities which exist in one network to a member of another." This type of network allows individuals to "get ahead" by being introduced to resources they might not otherwise have access to.

In order to successfully build bridging social capital an individual has to possess emotional intelligence. As they interact with individuals different from them culturally and economically, it is important to prioritize things like curiosity, conflict resolution, and cultural sensitivity.

Linking

The last type of social capital is linking. Claridge defines linking as a type of social capital that describes norms of respect and networks built of trusting relationships between people who interact *across* explicit, formal, or institutionalized *power or authority* gradients in society. Essentially, linking refers to navigating power dynamics and using them to one's advantage. In order to master linking social capital, we must recognize our own worth and know how to navigate interactions where individuals or groups may possess power over us. We need to learn to use our own power wisely and without abuse.

Below are the important elements families must address in order to assure strong social capital in future generations:

Bonding (strengthening connections)
Define your family's mission statement and values
Clarify family goals
Share family history
Discuss family secrets
Inquire about each family member's inner world
Practice compassion and affection for each other
Establish rituals

Bridging (resolving conflict, building openness to diversity)
Turn toward each other instead of away
Seek wise advisors
Solve your solvable problems
Acknowledge gridlock
Learn negotiation skills
Practice acceptance

Linking (master power dynamics)
Develop a healthy sense of self-worth
Understand your role within the family
Allow yourself to be influenced

Chapter Summary
In this chapter we explored the importance of social capital as well as ways our relationship-based resources can be disrupted. We learned that this primarily happens through a trauma related to our ability to form secure healthy attachments, creating a fear of abandonment. We explored abandonment wounds including personality disorders and some options for healing. We also looked at the three types of social capital and ways to strengthen those. Now it's time to move into reframing some of the thoughts underlying the *broken attachment* pain echo.

Reframing Our Pain
If you recall from Chapter Five, one technique used to address the language of inherited trauma is the "reframe". For reframes to be effective they must 1) feel true, and 2) bring emotional relief. This section offers examples of reframes for the *Broken Attachment* Pain Echo. Please remember if the revised statements do not meet these two criteria, we adjust them until they do.

The *Broken Attachment* Pain Echo
I need attention to feel valuable. - I know to be healthy I need a balance of earned worth and inherent worth. Earned worth is the good I do for my world. Inherent worth is the idea that I am valuable because I exist. I need both.
Shopping is how I relieve stress. - Although shopping relieves stress, I am working on other ways of relaxing.

If I were different people would like me better. - I am willing to practice acceptance over external validation.

I can be impulsive with my spending. - I can give myself a 24-hour window to think about this purchase.

I wish I could be confident about my decisions. - I am learning to be confident in my decisions.

My boss hates me. - I notice an extreme thought about my boss's perception of me. I wonder if it is true?

I'm not sure I know who I am. - I'm getting to know myself better. I know who I am.

My family ruined my life. - I am responsible for the outcomes in my life.

People say I'm unreliable. - I will take feedback from others and work to do better.

Why should I have to show up for people? They don't show up for me. - I believe showing up for people is important. However, I might overextend myself sometimes. I will work to set better boundaries.

Chapter Ten: Bankruptcy

The *Bankrupt* Pain Echo

I've lost so much.

I'm stuck and not making any progress.

Everyone takes advantage of me.

It takes so long to accomplish anything.

I'm terrified of the future.

I give up.

I just keep giving and don't get anything back.

There isn't enough.

I'm not enough.

My body has turned against me.

I can't trust myself.

bankrupt:
> 1. A person, business, or organization legally declared insolvent because of inability to pay debts.
>
> 2. A person who is totally lacking in a specified resource or quality.

If you made your way to this chapter, you or someone in your life might have found themselves at one of the lowest points in life. A recent tragedy or a slow cascade of unfortunate events in multiple areas of life, ranging from health issues to relationships and finances, leave life metaphorically (and sometimes literally) bankrupt. You or your loved one feel completely depleted and at a loss in terms of what to focus on or where to turn for help. The energy to keep going may feel like it's just not there. This chapter will explore some of the language commonly associated with a "bankrupt" life. I included two examples of issues in which I have seen extreme feelings of loss manifest: chronic illness and addictions. Note, these don't always occur in bankruptcy but reflect what I have witnessed in individuals and families.

I've Lost Everything: The Impact of Complex Grief on Family & Finances

Grief doesn't always look like grief. Sometimes it looks like chronic illness. March 3, 2014, I started exhibiting unexplained seizures that lasted nine days. Later, I discovered I contracted Lyme disease, leaving me severely disabled for four years. This diagnosis coincided with a very stressful work environment, the responsibility of helping care for my father during his cancer treatment, and a lawsuit from a business I had been involved in. While all these experiences were happening in my current life, I would later discover (and it would serve to be critical to my healing) uncanny overlaps between my family ancestors' lives. These overlaps included similar but more extreme circumstances of stressful work environments, cancer, and financial trauma.

After years of treatment, I returned to work and dedicated my therapy practice to assisting families suffering from Lyme and other chronic illnesses. Incredibly, time and again I observed the patterns of my clients' lives echo my own. Dejectedly, I witnessed entire lives fall apart, piece by piece, due to a number of unfortunate events completely draining them.

In Chinese medicine, Lyme disease is classified as a "gu" or what we refer to in Western medicine as a parasite. The parasitic energy of Lyme invaded not just the client's bodies but every aspect of their lives. Time and again, I saw bank accounts dwindle. Clients left abandoned by friends and spouses. I witnessed horrific lawsuits and theft by business partners. The similarities went beyond coincidence. I began referring to this as "the nature of Lyme disease." It seemed to just ruin everything.

In listening to clients suffering from Lyme disease, I noticed overlap between their internal stories and those of the clients I worked with in addiction recovery. Both types of clients were terrified of their future. They both expressed putting energy out, but little energy being returned to them. And they struggled with their relationship with money, regardless of socioeconomic status. Everything felt like a loss.

The Chronic Illness/Addiction Overlap
Loss related to chronic illness—including addictions—is a familiar theme across America. Somewhere between my graduation in 1998 and my sister's (2001), something went horribly wrong. It seemed every time we visited home we heard stories of the early demise of another one of my sister's classmates due to drug abuse. Our community was not the only one impacted by the opioid epidemic. According to NIDA, "drug overdose deaths in the U.S. involving heroin rose from 1,960 in 1999 to 15,482 in 2017 before trending down to 13,165 deaths in 2020 and 9,173 deaths in 2021".[39] Since then, drug overdoses have fluctuated up and down with overall drug overdose deaths rising again from 2019 to 2021. In 2021, 106,000 drug overdose deaths were reported.[40] Currently, 115 Americans die of opioid addiction daily in the United States.[41] For many families, these facts mean that an entire generation is lost who could otherwise participate in eldercare, parenting, and income creation. According to the nonprofit Eluna, the mission of which is to support children and families impacted by addiction,

> Substance use disorder is a tremendous stress on families, especially the most vulnerable members – the children. Their article, *Grandfamilies: Grandparents Raising Grandchildren Impacted by Addiction / Substance Use Disorder* states: "Some parents are forced to make tough decisions and turn to extended family to help raise their children. As of August 2018, there were more than one million grandchildren being raised by grandparents primarily due to the opioid epidemic in this country.[43]

How did we lose a generation? As a society, where were our blind spots? How can we heal from the grief and mitigate the impact on future generations? I believe, in the same way reframing personal narratives heals individuals, helping families express, heal, and reframe legacy narratives serves as a way to reclaim families and our communities from the loss associated with chronic illness, including addiction.

Both chronic mental and physical health issues including addictions pose many layers of threats which can drain family wealth and perpetuate a sense of loss including:

- Poor personal financial decision-making including irrational spending and gambling
- Manipulation or theft from family and friends

- Inability to maintain employment
- Increased medical expenses
- Broken relationships leading to lack of social support

One major factor in improving the lives of those living with or recovering from chronic issues is to address grief and loss. Let's take a look at some ways of beginning to address the experience of loss.

Addressing Inherited Complicated Grief
In my case and in the case of some individuals experiencing addiction there has been a major loss in the family narrative. As we learned from the first section these losses can include events like the tragic death of a loved one in earlier generations, the loss of financial status, loss of identity due to immigration, and loss of community due to war. As we can see, unresolved trauma and grief are intimately connected and can live on in the experiences of our children. In fact, those feelings of loss can continue to be acted out within the family system until resolved.

One way that grief can commonly occur in families is the tendency for a family to react to trauma or loss by ignoring it. In the ignoring, the family members involved can become emotionally frozen with unresolved grief around the issue. My grandmother, for example, had a child die in infancy. Rather than addressing her grief, she shifted her focus toward hypervigilance of her other children well into adulthood. The impact of hypervigilance on the second generation caused a host of different reactions in the third including generalized anxiety and drug use. This is a perfect example of how complicated grief once passed down generationally may not look or sound like grief at first glance. These complexities underscore why it is important to unpack family histories even when addressing seemingly unrelated current issues such as anxiety and substance use.

If we listen closely to the experiences of individuals with chronic illnesses (including use & abuse) we will inevitably hear the echoes of loss starting with their personal experiences. Often, someone will describe these losses in extremes. Either they will speak of the extreme loss as if it were not a big deal, minimizing and normalizing the experience or they will take the stance of the victim. In response to these stories, we can begin by reflecting and validating that they did, in fact, suffer a loss. Sometimes just having someone label it as such can lift us out of the haze of pain we often are not even aware we are living in. Group healing is great for labeling, hence being one of the most powerful ways to address loss. Whether it be an individual going to a group meeting for addictions, someone working through chronic illness finding others who have experienced the same thing, or a family coming together to mourn the loss of a loved one, the power of connection is invaluable in addressing loss.

The Power of Groups & Community for Healing Loss
In his most famous work, *Theory and Practice of Group Psychotherapy,* psychiatrist Irvin Yalom captures the essence and importance of group healing (this includes family therapy). Let's take a look at what Yalom has to say through his 12 therapeutic factors of collective/group healing:

1. **Instillation of hope**: One of the first things people learn from groups is that others have healed from inherited grief (or its manifestations).

2. **Universality**: It can feel incredibly lonely in grief. We can often look around and feel everyone else has moved on or is "just living their life." Groups help us know we are having a collective experience.

3. **Imparting information**: One of the most valuable ways groups helped me when I was sick was gaining insight from others who were a bit further along than I was.

4. **Altruism**: Groups help us find purpose outside ourselves and increase empathy.

5. **Corrective recapitulation of the primary family group:** To repeat if you haven't heard me emphasize it by now, families who venture into a process of healing together can completely transform their lives individually and collectively for generations.

6. **Development of socializing techniques:** Groups are a great place to practice social skills and the art of connection.

7. **Imitative behavior:** Modeling the healthy behaviors of others can alert us to inherited patterns we may not want to repeat.

8. **Interpersonal learning:** Our relationships help us learn exactly who we are and who we want to be. Groups are a great place to clarify values and practice expressing them.

9. **Group cohesiveness:** The sense of belonging we can get from groups is one remedy for the isolation epidemic.

10. **Catharsis:** At one point or another everyone needs a safe space to be fully seen and heard. Groups are a great place for this.

11. **Existential Factors:** Let's try not solving world peace on our own. Groups can help us contemplate life's big, difficult questions.

12. **Self-understanding:** What all this work is about; groups facilitate a deeper relationship with ourselves.[68]

It is important to note not all healing has to take place in the context of a "therapy" group. Other types of groups provide the above benefits. I encourage all individuals looking to heal from inherited patterns to enter into some form of collective support. That can look like peer groups, small groups associated with religious affiliation, masterminds, and retreats.

Industry Expert Insight

> Founder of Bespoke Addictions & Mental Health Treatment Center, Harbor, Paul Flynn highlights the importance of boundaries around money when working with addictions, chronic illness and mental health. He states it's important to be clear on your own legacy when thinking of financial support and inheritance planning for this population. He also shares that setting boundaries around financial support can reduce harm in the addicted or chronically ill loved one.

Chapter Summary
In this chapter we explored the concept of the *Bankrupt* pain Echo. We explored how inherited grief can be a catalyst for feelings of complete loss in multiple areas of life. This chapter also explored two common ways this can manifest, chronic mental and physical health issues, including addiction. This chapter also explored how powerful group and community-based interventions can be in healing this type of emotional pain Echo. Lastly, we gained insight from industry expert, Paul Flynn regarding the importance of boundary-setting from family members throughout the healing process. Lastly, let's review some supportive language and reframes to aid in repairing the *Bankrupt* pain echo.

Reframing Our Pain
If you recall from Chapter Five, one technique used to address the language of inherited trauma is the "reframe". For reframes to be effective they must 1) feel true, and 2) bring emotional relief. This section offers examples of reframes for the *Bankrupt* Pain Echo. Please remember if the revised statements do not meet these two criteria, we adjust them until they do.

The *Bankrupt* Pain Echo
I've lost so much. - Loss is painful. I'm allowed to take as long as I need to heal.

I'm stuck and not making any progress. - I made it through yesterday. I will make it through today.

Everyone takes advantage of me. - I notice an extreme thought about my interactions with others. I wonder if it is true?

It takes so long to accomplish anything. - Realistically, how far am I from finishing?

I'm terrified of the future. - My future is what I make it.

I give up. - Even though I feel like giving up, I will think about the reasons why I should keep going.

I just keep giving and don't get anything back. - Perhaps I should find a more constructive use of my energy.

There isn't enough. - What can I do with what I have?

I'm not enough. - What do I need to learn?

My body has turned against me. - What can I do to feel better?

I can't trust myself. - What can I do so I feel safe?

Part Three

Creating an ECHO Legacy™

In Part II, we dove into our echoes of pain. We explored some ways inherited trauma manifests in our daily lives and offered some solutions to begin addressing these. This section will incorporate the framework I created over my two decades of experience. In the same way I encourage individuals and families to clearly lay out their values and guiding principles, this section begins with mine - The ECHO Legacy™ Manifesto.

Thus, Part III, Creating an ECHO Legacy™ explains what to do with the excavated information and stories. This section describes the four pillars of the ECHO Legacy™ framework. It also offers practical action steps to begin building a stronger foundation which to discuss issues of money.

Chapter 11: One Solution

ECHO Legacy™ - The thoughtful, purpose-driven transmission of supportive traits & resources passed on to future generations.

In *It Didn't Start With You*, Mark Wolynn states: "Whether we inherit our emotions in the womb or they are transmitted in our early relationship with our mother, or we share them through unconscious loyalty or epigenetic changes, one thing is clear: life sends us forward with something unresolved from the past".[8] By exploring these unresolved feelings and patterns, we do not have to let them dictate our lives.

This chapter will review what I call the ECHO Legacy™ Manifesto, as well as its four pillars. The pillars include a section on why this element is fundamental to healing generational patterns, a case study, industry insights, and one primary action you can take today to improve this part of your family dynamic. Let's begin:

The ECHO Legacy Manifesto
- ECHO Legacies™ emphasize the present moment, encouraging family members to live the best they can, in the present moment.
- ECHO Legacies™ place heritage above inheritance. Due to this focus, they take time to collectively document and review key narratives and milestones within the family history for reflection and growth.
- ECHO Legacies™ value the idea of families being fully funded not just financially but also physically, intellectually, emotionally, socially, and spiritually. They place primary value on the growth of family members, prioritizing financial conversations. In doing so, family members trust the complications that wealth naturally resolves.
- ECHO Legacies™ acknowledge family members are heirs of great fortune regardless of economic status. Acknowledging this means we treat ourselves and our current resources with the highest respect and care.
- ECHO Legacies™ honor the spirit of the family while also remaining flexible to the changing needs of the future.
- When making decisions, ECHO Legacy™ creators take into account the reality that achievements and difficulties shape future generations.
- As ECHO Legacy™ inheritors, we acknowledge not all issues began with us and we work to let go of generational patterns that no longer serve us.

Developing an ECHO Legacy™ consists of 4 pillars:
- Effective Communication
- Compassion Driven Decision-Making

- Honoring of Resources
- Openness to Receiving

E- Effective Communication

The single biggest problem in communication is the illusion that it has taken place. -George Bernard Shaw

Effective communication is the primary pillar for success in your personal life, family, and community. I believe honoring our ancestors means living fully in the present moment, which includes being present in our communication. This book's key take-away regarding communication is that **effective communication is rooted in deep listening in the present moment.** Deep listening encourages interactions rooted in non-violence and compassion. For the benefit of ourselves and those we love, we must begin to **practice engaging in interactions that are non-violent today, even if everything from the past is not completely resolved.**

Understanding Nonviolent Communication

Created by psychologist Marshall Rosenberg, NVC is a language of compassion, used as a tool for positive social change, and as a spiritual practice. NVC is based on a fundamental principle:

"Underlying all human actions are needs that people are seeking to meet, and understanding and acknowledging these needs can create a shared basis for connection, cooperation, and more globally – peace."[45]

NVC reflects curiosity about unspoken, painful narratives those around us may be carrying. NVC provides the tools and consciousness to understand what triggers us, to take responsibility for our reactions, and to deepen our connection with ourselves and others, thereby transforming our habitual responses to life. Ultimately, it involves a radical change in how we think about life and meaning.

The following case study is an example of one family's transformation from harsh to nonviolent, compassionate communication. After the case study, we will examine the four parts of NVC in detail using the case study as an example.

Father-Daughter Case Study

"I don't care what you think about that," Alex bluntly stated to his daughter during multiple therapy meetings. Alex's personality was direct and clear. His daughter Ellen responded by bursting into tears, stating this type of communication made her feel devalued and unloved. Alex replied with: "I am just being honest. Don't take it personally." Ellen would look at me as if to say: "Please make him stop being so cruel to me."

Alex and Ellen came to me to work on Ellen's unwillingness to fulfill certain requirements in order to continue receiving funds from her parents. Twenty-eight and chronically ill, Ellen recently charged large amounts of medical bills on her parents' credit card without their full understanding or consent. Alex abandoned the idea of Ellen assuming control over the family accounting business and would now settle for not being taken advantage of financially.

An exploration of Alex's family history showed he came from what he described as a rigid, first-generation immigrant family of seven children. As the oldest child, Alex's mother had little time for him. Alex rarely mentioned his father. Ellen's mother, Alex's wife, was a stay-at-home mother. She played a passive role in major decisions for Ellen. She remained available to comfort Ellen if her father proved too "harsh or unreasonable."

At this point, I hope you spot some of the signs in communicating that might be linked to generational trauma. Did you catch any of these?

- Lack of empathy
- Difficulty hearing the other person's perspective
- Inability to set boundaries or defend oneself in a conversation
- Feeling powerless and as if one needs rescuing or saved from an interaction
- The mother's passive attitude and inability to mitigate the father's aggression

Inherited trauma places dysfunctional conversations on repeat. It allows families to say things like *"This is just how we are."* Essentially, we become cozy and familiar with very bad habits. Just because interactions always occur similarly doesn't constitute tradition. Shouldn't tradition have another standard, possibly one rooted in compassion and effectiveness? Nonviolent communication is central to effective communication. Let's examine what it takes to provide a safe environment to begin communicating nonviolently.

As a mediator, I started by providing a space which encouraged nonviolence. I did this by using the technique of *emotion validation*. I first began by validating both Alex and Ellen's experiences. To validate in therapy simply means to acknowledge the other person's perspective. Validating throughout the therapy process (and your family interactions) is so important; one article describes it as the underpinning of the therapy relationship.[44] I tend to agree. Validating someone's experience and emotions calms the anger center of the brain (amygdala) and allows for more connected interactions. The benefits include:

- Improving relationships
- Deescalating conflict
- Communicates that we are:
    - Listened to
    - Understood

- - Not being judged
- Allows for emotional space to disagree

Note I did not begin my interaction with Alex and Ellen by reviewing past arguments. I began in the present moment, acknowledging what is happening right there, in the room with the three of us. Validating can also work wonders in your interactions.

Validating
Positive psychology writer Jeremy Sutton, PhD has compiled an incredible list of ways we validate. Sutton's list below should be adopted by family members in their communication:

- Active listening – remaining focused, attentive, and *in the moment* while maintaining eye contact.
- *Mindfully responding* – monitoring verbal and nonverbal reactions to what is said.
- *Reflecting without judgment* – recognizing and verbalizing what the client is feeling (such as, "*I can see you are having a tough time at the moment*").
- *Being tolerant* – even if not in agreement with the client's behavior, consider their history and how their thoughts and feelings may make sense.
- *Demonstrating what they say is taken seriously*, such as acknowledging that something happening sounds awful, offering a tissue, or asking, "*What do you need right now*?" Acceptance throughout the session is crucial.
- *Restating what was said* – summarizing and simplifying what is said (verbally and nonverbally) by the client by providing accurate reflection (such as, "*You think it is unfair that you do all the housework, and you would like things to change.*")
- *Focusing on behaviors* – pointing out that the current behavior may be unhelpful and has not always worked in the past
- *Treating the person as an equal* – seeing the client as an equal and showing them the respect they deserve
- *Radical genuineness* – believing in the client's strengths and respecting that they are capable of change.[44]

But how can we validate our family members' perspectives if we feel they have hurt or disregarded our feelings? This is where nonviolent communication (NVC) comes in. Nonviolent communication requires us to make key changes in how we view interactions.

Nonviolent communication is made up of four parts:

1. Observation without judgment - We already discussed the importance of cultivating the ability to compassionately and nonjudgmentally, observe. This is also the first step in nonviolent communication. NVC encourages you to simply reflect back what you observe in the other person rather than placing any judgment on their actions or words.

2. Personal responsibility for your feelings - NVC states the actions of others is a *stimulus* to feelings, not a *cause*. When considered a stimulus, we have a choice in how we respond. Feelings often appear automatic and out of our control, thus practice is required. This practice also allows us to move out of a victim-frame mindset. By exerting control over our reactions, we no longer serve at the mercy of our loved ones and our emotions.

3. Connecting Emotions & Unmet Needs - In NVC the outer expression of emotions is an attempt to meet a need. Step three involves the practice of knowing what we need emotionally and stating them compassionately.

4. Making Requests - The last part is to practice making requests. Examples include: "I'd like for you to eat dinner with us." "I'd appreciate it if you would put your phone away while we talk."[46]

Mastering this step frees us from internalizing hurtful things or retaliating in some way. Instead, we ensure everyone involved has enough room for everyone's emotions

Industry Expert Insight

If you aren't sure where to start talking with your family about money, just start with having little bite-sized conversations. For example, if you are a couple, start having 15-minute budgeting conversations per week.- Chris Brophy, Financial Planning & Investment Associate at Goodpasture Gray in Nashville TN.

Effective (Nonviolent) Communication in Action

I Heard You Say…

Nonviolent communication is the most effective. It may not be easy. We may not like it, but it's a fact that when people feel safe, they are more receptive to what is being said.

I cannot tell you the amount of times family members come to therapy, talk *at* each other, and not remotely hear what the other person said. In order to master NVC we must first become experts at listening. The exercise below is my go-to tool for deep listening.

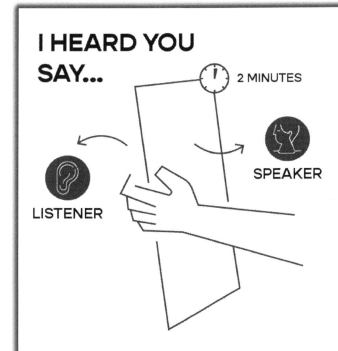

1. Use a double sided index card. One side says speaker, the other side says listener.
2. Allow the person with the speaker card facing them to speak for a designated time (say 2 minutes).
3. Once the speaker has finished speaking the listener is to ONLY respond with "I heard you say…" No other comment or dialogue is permitted.
4. The speaker then agrees that the listener heard correctly and continues for another two minutes. Or the speaker corrects the listener.
5. If the listener did not hear correctly they need to respond again with "I heard you say…"
6. Switch roles and repeat.

C - Compassionate Decision-Making

A healthy mind is one that can negotiate between the logical and emotional minds simultaneously. - Me

Compassionate decision-making is often hindered by an overlap between decision fatigue and burnout. Time and again families come to me because of resentments and feelings of being treated unfairly in family financial decisions. Many of these decisions are very complex. Family leaders must make decisions about managing or investing, deciding which heir will take over the family business, or complex decisions about estate planning. The one making the decisions can experience financial decision fatigue. This exhaustion can overlap with caregiver burnout. Caregiver burnout leads to a lack of empathy for those we care for resulting in careless, irrational decisions. The primary goal in my work with clients focuses on eliminating decision-making during an attitude of burnout or decision fatigue. **For the most effective compassionate decision-making, I advocate the simple but effective method of slowing down and clarifying your thoughts with a trusted neutral party.**

Soothe Emotions to Mitigate Relationship Risk
Much of my work revolves around role-playing to mitigate the risk of damaging relationships either through poor communication or poor decision-making. When stress becomes overwhelming, the mind generally tends to simplify things in order to make decisions. While this is a great energy saver for the brain, sometimes these simplifying decisions lack thoughtfulness and compassion.

Mitigating Risk Case Study
My client Ashlee called and said her family was in crisis. Her stepfather decided without the consent of her mother to sell their home in an effort to downsize. The 83-year-old already listed the home with a broker without considering the difficulty involved in attempting to find a suitable home for him and her mother. Additionally, the mother was scheduled for surgery in one month. Clearly, her mother needed a safe place to heal after surgery and without the stress of a move that she did not agree to. What happened to her stepfather's judgment? How could they stop the cascade of chaos given that all involved were adults with no obvious way to intervene?

More than just processing the stress of the situation (which was very important), my client needed real strategies to intervene on behalf of her parents. Luckily, Ashlee called upon a host of excellent advisors. She and her parents utilized a healthcare and legal advisory team both of her parents trusted. I supported Ashlee through the process of accessing these resources and diving to the root of her stepfather's hasty decision. Through many discussions, it came to light her stepfather struggled with grief combined with feeling extremely overwhelmed at managing her mother's health and the day-to-day maintenance of their home. Due to his stress, her stepfather failed to see his own cognitive distortion, resulting in black-and-white thinking. His attempt at simplification was a way to maintain his sanity during the upcoming perceived trials. The family developed a plan to provide him with more support, removed the house from the market, and everyone resumed normal life.

Ashlee and her family are an example of layers of decision-making done well.

- First, before her parents' health reached the point requiring critical attention, they put a healthcare team in place to address an emergency such as this.
- Second, they also invested in strong relationships with a legal team they trusted in times of stress.
- Third, Ashlee foresaw the damage of following her stepfather's lead on selling their home.
- Fourth, Ashlee initiated meaningful discussions about not only her emotions on the matter but a plan of action as well.

Ashlee did not engage in denial. She did not remain passive. She did not get angry and cause conflict with her stepfather. She remained calm and made the best possible decisions she could going forward to help her parents. These types of decisions help mitigate our own lapses in judgment, cognitive biases, and distortions.

Compassionate Decision-Making In Action

Steps to Assess Relationship Impact

Step I - Pick Your Trusted Advisor

The following are questions to consider when asking someone to assist with role play and mitigating risk in conversations.

Title	Role	Questions & Considerations
Mental Health Professional (LCSW, LMFT, LPC)	Specialize in mitigating the impact of emotional and behavioral reactions related to stress. Can possibly mediate in issues of divorce, parenting, couples, business partners, families. Equipped to address trauma and mental health diagnoses. If seeking someone with specialized knowledge in financial issues, their skills may be limited.	Have you helped mediate **X financial issues** in families before? How do you help individuals and families heal from generational patterns? How do you treat trauma? Do you work with families? Do you provide feedback during sessions or primarily listen?
Next Generation Advisor	Specialize in issues related to succession planning and next generation challenges related to inheritance or family enterprise responsibilities. Serve as mentor and advocate for next generation leaders. Offer educational opportunities for stewardship, estate planning, personal finance and taxes. Offer community and peer support.	Does the advisor have lived experience with wealth? If not, what makes them qualified? Can this advisor guide me on my own growth path without judgment?

Financial Therapist (CFT)	Specialize in the emotional challenges and barriers to sound financial decisions. Focus on building confidence and motivation to take control of and feel good about relationship with money.	Does the financial therapist specialize in your specific problem area? ie: financial trauma, fear of investing, challenges working with advisors, difficulty sticking to financial plans.
Financial Planner (CFP)	Specialized knowledge in sound investment decisions. Can assist with education around tools for sustaining and creating wealth.	Go to letsmakeaplan.org for a comprehensive guide on choosing a financial planner. How experienced is the CFP with family financial planning? Does the CFP have resources available if there is an issue outside their scope of practice?
Family Business Advisor	Specialize in helping families make sound decisions as a team. Usually have specific industry knowledge and can present possible scenarios based on years of experience.	Does this advisor have the specific experience we need at this phase of our business? Succession planning, leadership building, mediation, operations advising. What would be their process for helping make a decision which impacts the entire family system?

Estate Planner	Specialized knowledge in the areas of wills, trusts, and other tools for passing on wealth. May have a background in law and mediation depending on experience.	Check with friends and family for good referrals. Ask your financial planner if they know anyone with experience that fits your needs. Do they have a minimum of three years-experience? What is their experience with handling family conflict in the estate planning process?

Step II - Prepare to discuss the impact of this decision with your advisor.

The impact score is 1-5 (1 being minimal change/impact to individual or family system and 5 being extreme change/intense emotional or behavioral reaction)

Questions to discuss	Impact Score	Talking Points/Mitigation Plan
What do you want to see change?		
What is the impact? Relational/ Financial/ Emotional?		
How can you confirm everyone is clear on the outcome?		
How is the individual/ family/ community affected by this change?		
How do you anticipate them responding?		
How invested do you feel the i/f/c will be to make sure this happens?		

H - Honoring Resources

We are capable of infinitely more than we believe. We are stronger and more resourceful than we know, and we can endure much more than we think we can. David Blaine

Generational trauma, its roots held strongly in abuse and neglect, fractures a family's sense of honor.

Honor is both a noun and a verb and is defined as:
verb - 1a. to regard or treat (someone) with admiration and respect**:** to regard or treat with honor
b: to give special recognition to**:** to confer honor on
2 a: to live up to or fulfill the terms of
b: to accept as payment

noun 1a: good name or public esteem**:** REPUTATION
b: a showing of usually merited respect**:** RECOGNITION[16]

Creating an ECHO Legacy™ focuses on restoring honor to your family and resources no matter the challenges experienced. Families who succeed, place emphasis on the importance of the basics of respect for people and resources. One powerful way to accomplish this is by preserving and adding to family history. Throughout the ECHO Legacy™ process, we collect and sort through family stories, both uplifting and painful. We write them down. We look at how they impact our daily lives. And in some cases, we look at how to reframe our view of those stories in a way that adds meaning and value to the current generation. While looking at inherited patterns can feel overwhelming, we can approach them with patience and compassion. When addressed in this manner, family history preservation feels adventurous and creative. I have observed the process to be incredibly valuable for healing and cultivating family unity.

A primary principle of creating an ECHO Legacy™ is the ability to be forward-thinking while at the same time preserving our family's essence. The ECHO Legacy™ framework attempts to honor resources through a mindset shift rooted in the Japanese concept - *Mottainai,* meaning "it's a shame to waste". The word is a philosophy of approaching belongings with a sense of gratitude and humility, being mindful not to waste resources. Let's take a look at contrasting community views of resources.

Community Resource Case Study
At one time, West Virginia's forests were some of the most majestic on earth. The Central Appalachian Spruce Restoration Initiative documents the following:

On November 4, 1770, while traveling along the Kanawha River George Washington wrote in his journal, "Just as we came to the hills, we met with a Sycamore... of a most extraordinary size, it measuring three feet from the ground, forty-five feet round, lacking two inches; and not fifty yards from it was another, thirty-one feet round." As late as 1870, we read that "at least 10,000,000 acres (of the 16,640,000 acres of land in West Virginia) are still in all the vigor and freshness of original growth".

By the mid-1800s, West Virginia was in the midst of a logging boom that supplied the country with enough timber to build a 127-foot-wide boardwalk which could cover the circumference of the earth. Today, of the 10,000,000 acres of virgin forest existing before 1750, only 263 acres remain.[47]

Contrast this with the 14th-century logging practice still used in Japan today called *daisugi*. *Daisgui* translates to "platform cedar". Believed to have been created as a response to the need for lumber for tea room construction, the process allows for the roots and base trunk of a tree to be preserved. *Daisugi* applies bonsai pruning principles to full-scale logging and results in a harvest of straight logs that grow from the original trunk without cutting down the entire tree.[48,49] This process ensures the original trunk will keep producing for generations to come. How do you want to approach your family's legacy, strengths and resources? Through short term, gain of the current generation or with a broader view?

Honoring Resources in Action

We Are A Family Who...

One of the first exercises I do with families is a review of their values, mission, and collective actions. Complete the image below by choosing your family's core values from the list on the following page. Then, develop a collective family mission statement. Lastly, list out the actions you will complete which reflect your mission and values.

Mission, Vision, & Action Development can be used with:
Individuals
Marriages
Families
Family businesses/office
Community Organizations

Core Values List
Circle the top 3-5 values that describes you, your family or community

Authenticity	Creativity	Faith	Initiative	Respect
Adventure	Citizenship	Fame	Justice	Responsibility
Achievement	Community	Friendship	Joy	Risk-Taking
Ambition	Collaboration	Fun	Love	Service
Autonomy	Competence	Financial Stability	Loyalty	Success
Accountability	Determination	Gratitude	Leadership	Status
Balance	Diversity	Generosity	Learning	Teamwork
Beauty	Dignity	Growth	Meaningful work	Tradition
Belonging	Excellence	Gratitude	Nature	Travel
Boldness	Efficiency	Humor	Order	Thriftiness
Compassion	Equity	Honesty	Patience	Wealth
Career	Freedom	Health	Peace	Wisdom
Caring	Forgiveness	Intuition	Perseverance	Well-being

Mission Statement
An individual, family or community mission statement is a written declaration of the values you hold dear, the impact you hope to create in the world, and the deep connection you long for.[86]

Examples:
Individual - My mission is to serve as an educator in my community and to encourage those around me to live their best lives.

Family - We are a family who lovingly works together to make our home and community a better place.

Community - We are an organization who provides a safe, supportive, and inspiring space for its members in the hopes that every member can reach their full potential.

Write your mission statement here:

Actions

In this section, write the actions you will do individually or collectively which reflect your mission and values.

Examples:
Individual - I will write 3 books this year which provide education and uplifting material to families needing relationship support.

Family -
We will eat dinner together as a family every Thursday.
We will learn one new skill per month as a family.
We will volunteer in our community 3x this year as a family.

Community Organization -
We will meet monthly to discuss needs and follow up on goals for the community.
We will hold one yearly event aimed at building community and addressing isolation.
We will raise x amount of money to support 50 foster children in our community.

Write your actions here:

O - Openness to Receive

If your compassion does not include yourself, it is incomplete. — Jack Kornfield

The fourth pillar of creating an ECHO Legacy™ involves overcoming generational limitations to receiving all the good life, including money, can bring. Trauma's impact on feelings of gratitude, satisfaction, and fulfillment appears clear. Trauma increases the chances of negative emotional states, disrupting our ability to feel satisfaction on a daily basis.[50, 51] Trauma also causes us to over- or under-react to stimulus, diminishing our ability to "like and want" things in the future. Immediately after a trauma, survivors experience feelings of numbness and use phrases like "I don't feel like myself" and "I don't think I will ever be able to feel again." Knowing these responses, we understand why trauma survivors never want to experience another surprise in their life. One surprise I see often is the unexpectedness of sudden wealth such as an unknown inheritance or a sudden increase in earnings. Rather than accepting and using the new resources, generational trauma can result in feelings of shock and overload leading to poor decision-making. Essentially, trauma shuts down the parts of our brain involved in enjoying the present moment, celebrating successes, as well as feeling positive emotions like gratitude and awe.[51] Practicing an openness to receive is a way to reclaim joy in the unexpected.

The Glass Castle - A story of surprises

Sometimes money comes with a lot of unresolved emotional needs, such as anger, lack of understanding, and resentment. Take the true story of author Jeanette Walls. In her book *The Glass Castle,* Walls recounts a childhood of chaos and poverty growing up in Welch, WV. Determined to live a successful life, Walls leaves home and moves to New York City to pursue a career in writing. As her life progresses, her parents' mental health deteriorates. Her father and mother eventually move to New York City where they live out their lives in and out of homeless shelters. The twist of this story comes at the end. Jeanette discovers her parents owned a ranch out west worth well over $1 million. Appalled at the fact her father neglected their basic needs as children, Walls cuts off contact with her father. After her father's passing, Walls and her siblings finally find peace with their parents' mental illness and alcohol abuse. They also discover ways to collectively use their resources to better their own lives and inspire others.

Although not a formal diagnosis, the experience of being unprepared for and receiving sudden wealth is called sudden wealth syndrome (SWS). According to Investopedia, "SWS is characterized by isolation from former friends, guilt over their change in circumstances, and extreme fear of losing their money."[52] When I explain to individuals

I work with "Sudden Wealth Syndrome" the response is generally," I wish I had that problem!" followed by intense laughter. My next response is generally, "Well no, actually you don't wish you had that problem because it means you are not ready to manage sudden wealth and you suffer from other issues which need to be addressed in order to maintain your new financial status. Otherwise, like 33% of lottery winners, you may end up filing for bankruptcy within five years.[62]

The root of all three issues derives from a confused or limited sense of self. When we build strong relationships and surround ourselves with individuals who genuinely care about us, the issue of isolation from friends becomes irrelevant. When we possess a strong sense of self and clear understanding of our dreams, we understand money is a tool to be used in our lives to fulfill those desires. With confidence in our ability to constantly create and manage money (or at least the confidence to find trusted counsel), we will never worry about losing it.

Some surprises can be tragic. We suffer accidents, receive unexpected tax bills, or become blindsided by the behaviors of loved ones. Family financial surprises cannot always be clearly defined as good or bad. They bring a complex mix of responsibilities, excitement, hurt feelings, and relief. From the outside, most people view these as purely positive. On the receiving end, many layers of stressful emotions and stories connect to the money.

Industry Expert Insight

> *Growing up, my family's relationship with wealth felt like being caught in a "money sprinkler"—sporadic bursts of financial generosity with no clear pattern, dictated entirely by someone else's whims. It wasn't something we controlled, and that lack of control shaped much of my early relationship with money. My grandparents, who held the wealth, would occasionally shower us with extravagant experiences… but these moments were scattered and unpredictable. The result was a confusing mix of material comfort without any sense of ownership or security. The unpredictability of the money sprinkler fostered what I call "money dysmorphia." I knew we were theoretically wealthy, but it didn't feel like our wealth. This feeling of being a "conspicuous fraud" stayed with me into adulthood. As I grew older, the hunger for wealth quieted down, but it didn't disappear. I became more pragmatic, realizing that building a career and financial stability is a decades-long process, and that I'm unlikely to ever live the life my grandfather did. - Torri Hawley, G7 Family Shareholder*

If we compare the symptoms of trauma with the emotion of surprise, trauma can be explained as surprise's most extreme and painful expression. Essentially, trauma entails the worst of all parts of a surprise, state of shock and feeling blind-sided. Science supports the brain's need to be in what I call "surprise rich" environments. In their book, *Surprise: Embrace the Unpredictable and Engineer the Unexpected*, Tania Luna and Leeann Renninger argue surprises bring vitality to our lives. Trauma causes us to be "surprise adverse". Luna and Renninger point out the transformative effects of surprise. In her Ted Talk, Luna discusses leaning into the unexpected, facilitating her own healing from early childhood traumas. She describes small everyday surprises as an opportunity to pause and appreciate life in new ways. She cites research on monkeys indicating we appreciate surprise gifts more fully than expected ones. We also remember surprises better than repetitive daily interactions. Luna states it is not helpful to cling to daily routines. As a resilience practice, she urges us to step out of our comfort zones. She lists some tips to practice:

- Look at any moment which is dull, lonely, frustrating, or unfulfilling. What can I do right now that is surprising?
- Create pattern interrupts, such as testing out new ways of handling conflict.
- Ask yourself, "What can I do right now that's surprising?"
- Switch up an aspect of your daily routine.
- Seek novelty/try new things.
- Take positive risks.
- Face a fear.
- Surprise others[4, 63, 64, 65, 66, 67]

Openness to Receive in Action

I Remember A Time When…

The exercise below is one I use with individuals and clients to help them find what hypnotherapists refer to as source memories. These memories can serve as a reminder to be open to the good things life has to offer us today. Fill out the sheet below(as an individual, family or community) and use it as a discussion starter.

I remember a time when I felt deeply connected to nature….

I remember a time when I accepted myself fully….

I remember a time when I appreciated where I came from…

I remember a time when I was able to forgive…

I remember a time when I laughed really hard…

I remember a time when I felt tremendous gratitude…

I remember a time when I enjoyed silence…

I remember a time when I allowed myself to be spontaneous…

I remember a time when I fully felt pain…

Conclusion

In creating the definition of an ECHO Legacy™ I spent time reflecting on my personal experiences of inherited financial trauma as well as my professional work over the past twenty years. I reflected on navigating my own inherited memories, the overlap between my experience with chronic illness, and the financial behaviors that, by no fault of my own, I was born into. As a therapist and consultant, I have had the pleasure of working with thousands of individuals and families from a variety of economic and cultural backgrounds. It has been exciting to watch family businesses and offices experience pattern breaking "aha" moments, making stronger connections and creating a greater impact on their community.

Culturally, we have reached a turning point where we can no longer deny the impact of past generations' mistakes affecting our present experiences. Modern life is full of polarity, irrationality, separation, and distraction. Despite my optimism, it is clear succession and inheritance planning is still a taboo topic in many households. In this book, I attempted to help start a dialogue on the subject in a spirit of encouragement toward compassionate communication. By slowing down and listening carefully to family narratives, we begin to separate what we want to echo into future generations and what we can lovingly let pass away. The framework I have provided will help you and your family to identify your values and set you up for success.

I also hope you developed an increased willingness and confidence in your ability to look at difficult topics individually and as a family. Perhaps, you are ready to take small steps toward reconnecting with ancestors through genealogy research, family audits or new rituals. Possibly, you feel a deeper sense of connection toward the loved ones who have passed and those currently in your life. Hopefully, you are making relationships more of a priority.

Contrary to popular belief, legacies are not just static abstracts, names on buildings, or pots of money passed down to the next generation. Legacies include layers of our own experiences combined with the echoes of our ancestors'. They reflect the culmination of decisions made by ourselves and the generations before us. Within the first section, we explored how we came to view succession and inheritance through the lens of denial.

We explored the epigenetic impact of trauma on our day to day lives, including its impact on health and relationships. We examined how generational family trauma shapes our money scripts and internal narratives. We learned these early childhood narratives shape the way we interact with money throughout our lifespan. We also explored the state of the modern family and how maintaining deep relationships has grown increasingly complex. Those complexities include an increase in divorce and blended families, relocation and distance, reduction in family quality time (including rituals like sharing mealtime) as well as the influence of technology on the family system. Collectively, we are in the midst of "the great wealth transfer" and many younger adults feel unprepared emotionally and educationally to handle their inheritance. As a result, more attention needs to be paid to purposeful planning on both the family leader side and the side of next generation inheritors.

In Part Two, I gently encouraged you and your family to begin looking at difficult subjects in your family history. As generations pass away, inevitably old wounds will arise and linger. Left unaddressed, they prove extremely destructive to individuals, families and family businesses. I encouraged you to look for blind spots where trauma intentionally closed you off from something requiring attention. I suggested addressing these blind spots through a family audit conducted with a therapist, coach or consultant. The assessment I created encompasses four areas from which to gauge your success in raising a family prepared to earn and preserve true wealth.

The first category pertains to security. Everyone needs spaces and relationships allowing us to feel safe. Security comes from within, meaning our self-image. It also comes from our environment, including the trust cultivated in relationships, beginning with family.

The second category relates to emotional currency and relates to how well we utilize emotions to our benefit. We are not prisoners to trauma. We must not pathologize everything. Complete and total healing is possible for ourselves and our communities. We discussed the topic of Post Traumatic Growth, transforming traumas into growth opportunities.

The third category, understanding options, highlighted the desperate state of irrationality and lack of critical thinking present in our lives. We looked at how inherited trauma plays a part in our day-to-day thoughts and behaviors and the need to practice critical thinking. Trauma's impact on rational decision-making is most apparent by its disruption to executive function skills including our memory recall, organizing, and the ability to follow through with projects.

The fourth category, social capital, emphasizes the importance of cultivating strong social connections with our families as the place to start. We reviewed how generational trauma impacts our ability to engage with the community, including causing lack of trust and avoidance. Generational trauma lowers our ability to participate on teams and impedes leadership skills through low self-esteem and lack of motivation. The last category, emotional bankruptcy, focuses on what happens when life circumstances become completely overwhelming. We reviewed two examples of what can occur simultaneously to financial disasters. Chronic health issues including substance abuse issues can cause or perpetuate financial trauma. And at the root of both issues is a sense of intense loss and insecurity. In this chapter I proposed the community/group healing model as an effective way to address this issue.

Throughout this section, you were prompted to take the assessment provided to determine areas of strength and areas needing improvement in your journey to healing from generational trauma.

In Part Three I introduced you to the ECHO Legacy™ Manifesto. This philosophy includes striving to create a legacy done well, putting heritage above inheritance, and fostering a belief in family members that we can be fully funded in all areas of our lives. Creating an ECHO Legacy™ also acknowledges our experiences significantly impact future generations and creating an ECHO Legacy™ begins in the present moment.

I define ECHO Legacy™ as: the thoughtful, purpose-driven transmission of supportive traits and resources passed on to future generations. The "ECHO" in ECHO Legacy™ stands for:

- Effective Communication
- Compassionate Decision-Making
- Honoring of Resources
- Openness to Receiving

After gleaning an understanding of ECHO Legacy™, you may harbor thoughts about your family history and your own blind spots. I suggest you start by taking the following actions:

- Connect with me. Share your ideas on legacy creation. I'd love to hear from you.
- Start a conversation. Use this book as a conversation starter with your family, advisor, therapist, or community.
- Sign up for my ECHO Legacy™ Newsletter to follow the conversation.
- Book an audit for you or your family business.

Acknowledgements

The journey to this book's publication has been over twenty years in the making. Along this journey I have been blessed to have learned from amazing mentors. I have had the privilege of learning resilience, creativity and tenacity from the clients I have served over these years. In writing this book I also had the pleasure of interviewing and learning from amazing thought leaders in the fields of psychology, estate planning, finance, and spirituality. To everyone who contributed to this project and supported me along the way, I want to say thank you.

A big thank you also to Diane Cady and Lorretta Smith for keeping me on track every step of the way.

I also want to thank my husband, Anu, for supporting me over the past year and a half as this project has come to life.

Bibliography

1. Cerulli and Associates. (2022, January 20). *Press Release: Cerulli Anticipates $84 Trillion in Wealth… Cerulli.* Retrieved August 15, 2024, from Cerulli Associates: https://www.cerulli.com/press-releases/cerulli-anticipates-84-trillion-in-wealth-transfers-through-2045
2. McKinsey & Co. (2022, February 16). *Agendas for best wealth management growth.* Retrieved August 15, 2024, from McKinsey & Company: https://www.mckinsey.com/industries/financial-services/our-insights/us-wealth-management-a-growth-agenda-for-the-coming-decade
3. Synergeticplaytherapy.com. (2023, November 18). *Explicit Memory versus Implicit Memory: When Do Kids Remember?* Retrieved October 22, 2024, from Synergetic Play Therapy Institute: https://synergeticplaytherapy.com/explicit-memory-versus-implicit-memory-kids-remember/
4. Luna, T. (n.d.). *TED Talks.* Retrieved August 26, 2024, from Tania Luna: https://www.tanialuna.com/talks
5. Matousek, M. (2016, June 23). *It Didn't Start With You: The Mystery of Inherited Trauma.* Retrieved August 16, 2024, from Psychology Today: https://www.psychologytoday.com/intl/blog/ethical-wisdom/201606/it-didnt-start-you-the-mystery-inherited-trauma
6. Yehuda, R., & Lehrner, A. (2018, September 7). *Intergenerational transmission of trauma effects: putative role of epigenetic mechanisms.* Retrieved August 16, 2024, from NCBI: https://www.ncbi.nlm.nih.gov/pmc/articles/PMC6127768/#wps20568-bib-0093
7. OConnell, K. (2015, August 27). *Native Americans Have 'Always Known': Science Has Proved Genetic Inheritance of Trauma.* Retrieved August 16, 2024, from Shadow Proof: https://shadowproof.com/2015/08/27/native-americans-have-always-known-science-proves-genetic-inheritance-of-trauma/
8. Wolynn, M. (2017). *It Didn't Start with You: How Inherited Family Trauma Shapes Who We Are and How to End the Cycle.* Penguin Publishing Group.
9. Lowe, T. (2021, February 26). *What is 'community' and why is it important?* Retrieved August 16, 2024, from Centre For Public Impact (CPI): https://www.centreforpublicimpact.org/insights/what-is-community-and-why-is-it-important
10. Johnson, R. (n.d.). *How Healthy Is McDowell County, West Virginia? | US News Healthiest Communities.* Retrieved August 16, 2024, from USNews.com: https://www.usnews.com/news/healthiest-communities/west-virginia/mcdowell-county
11. Towell, L., Haselby, S., Saunt, C., & Photos, M. (2015, January 7). *How were 1.5 billion acres of land so rapidly stolen?* Retrieved August 16, 2024, from Aeon: https://aeon.co/essays/how-were-1-5-billion-acres-of-land-so-rapidly-stolen
12. Downtown Alliance. (2021, January 28). *The Slave Market At Pearl Street And Wall Street.* Retrieved August 16, 2024, from Downtown Alliance: https://downtownny.com/news/black-gotham-experience-slave-market-pearl-wall-street/
13. Nicolaci da Costa, P. (2019, September 3). *America's First Bond Market Was Backed By Enslaved Human Beings.* Retrieved August 16, 2024, from Forbes: https://www.forbes.com/sites/pedrodacosta/2019/09/01/americas-first-bond-market-was-backed-by-enslaved-human-beings/?sh=711913ec1888

14. NABA. (2023, March 23). *Why Diversity in Finance Matters.* Retrieved August 16, 2024, from Forbes: https://www.forbes.com/sites/forbeseq/2023/03/23/why-diversity-in-finance--business-matter/?sh=cf796a9498a6
15. Lake, R., Perez, Y., & Gratton, P. (2024, August 13). *The Financial Advisor Profession Still Lacks Diversity.* Retrieved August 16, 2024, from Investopedia: https://www.investopedia.com/financial-advisor/fa-profession-accountable-lack-diversity/
16. Merriam-Webster's Dictionary. (n.d.). *Honor Definition & Meaning.* Retrieved August 26, 2024, from Merriam-Webster: https://www.merriam-webster.com/dictionary/honor
17. *3 Reasons Why Diversity and Inclusion are Important for the Financial Planning Profession.* (2020, March 30). Retrieved August 16, 2024, from CFP Board: https://www.cfp.net/knowledge/industry-insights/2020/03/3-reasons-why-diversity-and-inclusion-are-important-for-the-financial-planning-profession
18. Asare, J. G. (2022, February 14). *3 Ways Intergenerational Trauma Still Impacts the Black Community Today.* Retrieved August 17, 2024, from Forbes: https://www.forbes.com/sites/janicegassam/2022/02/14/3-ways-intergenerational-trauma-still-impacts-the-black-community-today/?sh=a81d9d03cf68
19. Kahler, R., & Fox, K. (2005). *Conscious Finance: Uncover Your Hidden Money Beliefs and Transform the Role of Money in Your Life.* FoxCraft.
20. Klontz, B. (2018, June 6). *Money Scripts: The Psychology of Wealth.* Retrieved August 17, 2024, from Youtube: https://www.youtube.com/watch?v=fx3O3fLJRE8
21. Klontz, B. (2015). *Klontz Money Scripts Test.* Retrieved August 17, 2024, from Dr. Brad Klontz: https://www.bradklontz.com/moneyscriptstest
22. Morgan, A. (2000, December 1). *Free Extract from Alice Morgan's 'What is Narrative Therapy?'.* Retrieved August 17, 2024, from The Dulwich Centre: https://dulwichcentre.com.au/what-is-narrative-therapy/
23. Airica, L. (2023, February 13). *The Power, Influence and ENERGY OF WORDS.* Retrieved October 2024, from YouTube: https://www.youtube.com/watch?v=vkA-EOJ_iBU
24. God, A. (1611-1999). *The Holy Bible: King James Version.* Viking Studio. Retrieved from https://quod.lib.umich.edu/cgi/k/kjv/kjv-idx?type=DIV1&byte=1477#:~:text=1,the%20face%20of%20the%20waters.
25. Paul, M. (2012, September 19). *Your Memory is like the Telephone Game.* Retrieved August 21, 2024, from Northwestern Now: https://news.northwestern.edu/stories/2012/09/your-memory-is-like-the-telephone-game
26. Bridge, D., & Paller, K. (2012, August 29). *Neural Correlates of Reactivation and Retrieval-Induced Distortion.* Retrieved August 21, 2024, from The Journal of Neuroscience: https://www.jneurosci.org/content/32/35/12144.abstract
27. Carlson, R. (1997). *Slowing Down to the Speed of Life: How to Create a More Peaceful, Simpler Life from the Inside Out.* HarperSanFrancisco.
28. Brown, B. (2013, January 15). *Shame vs. Guilt - Brené Brown.* Retrieved August 21, 2024, from Brene Brown: https://brenebrown.com/articles/2013/01/15/shame-v-guilt/
29. Wikipedia. (n.d.). *Pudendal nerve.* Retrieved August 21, 2024, from Wikipedia: https://en.wikipedia.org/wiki/Pudendal_nerve
30. American Psychological Association. (n.d.). *Reparenting.* Retrieved August 22, 2024,

from APA Dictionary: https://dictionary.apa.org/reparenting
31. LePera, N. (2021). *How to Do the Work: Recognize Your Patterns, Heal from Your Past, and Create Your Self.* HarperCollins Publishers.
32. Housel, M. (2020). *The Psychology of Money: Timeless Lessons on Wealth, Greed, and Happiness.* (M. Housel, Ed.) Harriman House.
33. Shin, L. M., Rausch, S. L., & Pitman, R. K. (2006, July). *Amygdala, medial prefrontal cortex, and hippocampal function in PTSD.* Retrieved August 22, 2024, from PubMed: https://www.youtube.com/watch?v=XgSOuFTXALg&t=66s
34. Memory and Aging Center. (n.d.). *Executive Functions.* Retrieved August 22, 2024, from UCSF: Weill Institute for Neurosciences: https://www.youtube.com/watch?v=XgSOuFTXALg&t=66s
35. Hughes, J. E. (2004). *Family Wealth: Keeping It in the Family--How Family Members and Their Advisers Preserve Human, Intellectual, and Financial Assets for Generations.* Wiley.
36. Chan, J. C., Nugent, B. M., & Bale, T. L. (2017, October 13). *Parental Advisory: Maternal and Paternal Stress Can Impact Offspring Neurodevelopment.* Retrieved August 22, 2024, from Biological Psychiatry: https://www.biologicalpsychiatryjournal.com/article/S0006-3223(17)32061-9/abstract
37. Claridge, T. (2016, December 13). *Examples of social capital • Institute for Social Capital.* Retrieved August 22, 2024, from Institute for Social Capital: https://www.socialcapitalresearch.com/examples-social-capital/
38. Collier, L. (2016, November). *Growth after trauma.* Retrieved August 22, 2024, from American Psychological Association: https://www.biologicalpsychiatryjournal.com/article/S0006-3223(17)32061-9/abstract
39. National Institute on Drug Abuse. (2024, August). *Drug Overdose Deaths: Facts and Figures.* Retrieved August 23, 2024, from NIDA.NIH.GOV | National Institute on Drug Abuse (NIDA): https://nida.nih.gov/research-topics/trends-statistics/overdose-death-rates
40. Thatcher, C. (2021, June 17). *Writing can improve mental health – here's how.* Retrieved August 22, 2024, from The Conversation: https://theconversation.com/writing-can-improve-mental-health-heres-how-162205
41. American Addiction Centers. (2024, May 3). *A Decade of American Drug Use.* Retrieved August 23, 2024, from DrugAbuse.com: https://drugabuse.com/featured/a-decade-of-american-drug-use/
42. Claridge, T. (2018, January 6). *What is Bonding Social Capital?* Retrieved August 22, 2024, from Institute for Social Capital: https://www.socialcapitalresearch.com/what-is-bonding-social-capital/
43. Callentine, P., Bristol, M., & Nugent, R. (n.d.). *Grandfamilies: Grandparents Raising Grandchildren Impacted by Addiction / Substance Use Disorder.* Retrieved August 23, 2024, from Eluna Network: https://elunanetwork.org/resources/grandfamilies-grandparents-raising-granchildren-impacted-by-addiction-subst
44. Sutton, J., & Neuhaus, M. (2021, September 1). *What Is Validation in Therapy & Why Is It Important?* Retrieved August 24, 2024, from PositivePsychology.com: https://positivepsychology.com/validation-in-therapy/#psychology

45. Kashtan, I., & Kashtan, M. (n.d.). *Basics of Nonviolent Communication – BayNVC.* Retrieved August 24, 2024, from BayNVC: https://baynvc.org/basics-of-nonviolent-communication/
46. Rosenberg, M. B. (2015). *Nonviolent Communication: A Language of Life: Life-Changing Tools for Healthy Relationships (Non-violent Communication Guides).* Puddledancer Press.
47. Saville, D. (2012, May 25). *Logging the Virgin Forests of West Virginia – Page 2 – CASRI.* Retrieved August 26, 2024, from Central Appalachian Spruce Restoration Initiative: https://restoreredspruce.org/2012/05/25/logging-the-virgin-forests-of-west-virginia/2/
48. Utaraitė, N., Wilson, S., & Nunya, M. (2020, July 30). *Apparently, This Ancient Japanese Technique From The 14th Century Allows People To Produce Lumber Without Having To Cut Down Trees.* Retrieved August 26, 2024, from Bored Panda: https://www.boredpanda.com/sustainable-japanese-forestry-daisugi/?utm_source=en.wikipedia&utm_medium=referral&utm_campaign=organic
49. Sataksig. (2020, July 10). *Daisugi, The Ancient Bonsai Technique That Can Prevent Deforestation.* Retrieved August 26, 2024, from Earthbuddies: https://earthbuddies.net/daisugi
50. Nicolson, N. A. (2018, August 31). *The Relative Impact of Traumatic Experiences and Daily Stressors on Mental Health Outcomes in Sri Lankan Adolescents.* Retrieved August 26, 2024, from NCBI: https://www.ncbi.nlm.nih.gov/pmc/articles/PMC6174989/
51. Fonzo, G. A. (2018, October 21). *Diminished positive affect and traumatic stress: A biobehavioral review and commentary on trauma affective neuroscience.* Retrieved August 26, 2024, from NCBI: https://www.ncbi.nlm.nih.gov/pmc/articles/PMC6234277/
52. Chen, J., & Howard, E. (n.d.). *Sudden Wealth Syndrome (SWS): Definition, Causes, and Treatment.* Retrieved August 27, 2024, from Investopedia: https://www.investopedia.com/terms/s/suddenwealthsyndrome.asp
53. Simon, T. (2024). *Mark Wolynn: Becoming Aware of Inherited Family Trauma.* Retrieved September 23, 2024, from Sounds True: Mark Wolynn: Becoming Aware of Inherited Family Trauma
54. Rechavi, O., & Lev, I. (2017, July 24). *Principles of Transgenerational Small RNA Inheritance in C. elegans.* Retrieved September 23, 2024, from Science Direct.Com: https://www.sciencedirect.com/science/article/pii/S0960982217305791
55. Painter, S., & Dutton, D. G. (1993). *Emotional attachments in abusive relationships: a test of traumatic bonding theory.* Retrieved September 23, 2024, from PubMed: https://pubmed.ncbi.nlm.nih.gov/8193053/
56. Woodard, B. (2020, March 2). *The First National Bank of Keystone Scandal.* Retrieved September 24, 2024, from Clio: https://theclio.com/entry/94923
57. Summers, J., Acovino, V., & Intagliata, C. (2023, May 2). *America has a loneliness epidemic. Here are 6 steps to address it.* Retrieved September 24, 2024, from NPR: https://www.npr.org/2023/05/02/1173418268/loneliness-connection-mental-health-dementia-surgeon-general

58. Hawkley, L. C., Zheng, B., & Song, X. (2020, June). *Negative Financial shock increases loneliness in older adults.* Retrieved September 24, 2024, from ScienceDirect: https://www.sciencedirect.com/science/article/abs/pii/S0277953620302197?via%3Dihub
59. Mahalakshmi, S. (2024, August 30). *Matrika, Mātṛkā, Mātṛka, Mātrikā: 30 definitions.* Retrieved September 30, 2024, from Wisdom Library: https://www.wisdomlib.org/definition/matrika
60. Myers, M. (2023, November 21). *e-WV | McDowell County.* Retrieved October 1, 2024, from The West Virginia Encyclopedia: https://www.wvencyclopedia.org/articles/1631
61. Sawhill, I. V. (2020, July 20). *Sawhill_Social Capital_Final.* Retrieved October 2, 2024, from Brookings Institution: https://www.brookings.edu/wp-content/uploads/2020/07/Sawhill_Social-Capital_Final_07.16.2020.pdf
62. Ranzetta, T. (2023, January 18). *What percent of lottery winners eventually go bankrupt? - Blog.* Retrieved October 8, 2024, from Next Gen Personal Finance: https://www.ngpf.org/blog/question-of-the-day/question-of-the-day-what-percent-of-lottery-winners-eventually-go-bankrupt/
63. Trafton, A. (2019, July 15). *How expectation influences perception.* Retrieved October 8, 2024, from Science Daily: https://www.sciencedaily.com/releases/2019/07/190715114249.htm
64. Princeton University. (2020, November 25). *Basketball on the brain: Neuroscientists use sports to study surprise.* Retrieved October 8, 2024, from Science Daily: https://www.sciencedaily.com/releases/2020/11/201125114346.htm
65. Krauss, S. (2022, April 2). *The Unexplored Emotion of Surprise.* Retrieved October 8, 2024, from Psychology Today: https://www.psychologytoday.com/us/blog/fulfillment-any-age/202204/the-unexplored-emotion-surprise
66. Kanter, R. M. (2013, July 17). *Surprises Are the New Normal; Resilience Is the New Skill.* Retrieved October 8, 2024, from Harvard Business Review: https://hbr.org/2013/07/surprises-are-the-new-normal-r
67. Suttie, J. (2015, April 24). *Why Humans Need Surprise | Greater Good.* Retrieved October 8, 2024, from Greater Good Science Center: https://greatergood.berkeley.edu/article/item/why_humans_need_surprise
68. Yalom, I. D., & Leszcz, M. (2008). *The Theory and Practice of Group Psychotherapy.* Basic Books.
69. Becker, N. V. (2022, August 22). *Association of Chronic Disease With Patient Financial Outcomes Among Commercially Insured Adults.* Retrieved October 8, 2024, from NCBI: https://www.ncbi.nlm.nih.gov/pmc/articles/PMC9396471/
70. Merriam Webster Dictionary. (2024, October 14). *Wealth Definition & Meaning.* Retrieved October 21, 2024, from Merriam-Webster: https://www.merriam-webster.com/dictionary/wealth
71. Ablison. (n.d.). *Pros and Cons of Gamification.* Retrieved October 23, 2024, from ablison.com: https://www.ablison.com/pros-and-cons-of-gamification/
72. Mackintosh, P. (2018, October 19). *Generational Wealth: Why do 70% of Families Lose Their Wealth in the 2nd Generation?* Retrieved October 21, 2024, from Nasdaq (101): https://www.nasdaq.com/articles/generational-wealth%3A-why-do-70-of-fami-

lies-lose-their-wealth-in-the-2nd-generation-2018-10

73. Perry, A. M., & Stephens, H. (2024, January 9). *Black wealth is increasing, but so is the racial wealth gap.* Retrieved October 21, 2024, from Brookings Institution: https://www.brookings.edu/articles/black-wealth-is-increasing-but-so-is-the-racial-wealth-gap/

74. Kennedy, J. H., & Kennedy, C. E. (2004, January 2). *Attachment theory: Implications for school psychology.* Retrieved October 22, 2024, from Wiley Online Library: https://onlinelibrary.wiley.com/doi/10.1002/pits.10153

75. The Attachment Project. (n.d.). *Attachment Disorders: Causes, Types and Symptoms - AP.* Retrieved October 21, 2024, from Attachment Project: https://www.attachment-project.com/psychology/attachment-disorders/

76. National Park Service. (2021, August 8). *Homesteading by the Numbers - Homestead National Historical Park (U.S.* Retrieved October 22, 2024, from National Park Service: https://www.nps.gov/home/learn/historyculture/bynumbers.htm

77. Peyton, S. (2020, January 23). *Healing Addiction With Unconscious Contract Work.* Retrieved October 22, 2024, from Sarah Peyton: https://sarahpeyton.com/addiction-unconscious-contracts/

78. Ellis, G., Voelkl, J., & Morris, C. (1994). *Measurement and analysis issues with explanation of variance in daily experience using the flow model.* Retrieved October 23, 2024, from Journal of Leisure Research: https://psycnet.apa.org/record/1995-23850-001

79. Bevelin, P., & guide, s. (n.d.). *Mental Models: Learn How to Think Better and Gain a Mental Edge.* Retrieved October 23, 2024, from James Clear: https://jamesclear.com/mental-models

80. Stamper, J. (2024, October 21). *Gamification Definition & Meaning.* Retrieved October 23, 2024, from Merriam-Webster: https://www.merriam-webster.com/dictionary/gamification

81. NeuroLaunch. (2024, October 1). *Laundry Therapy: Transform Chores into Self-Care Rituals.* Retrieved October 23, 2024, from NeuroLaunch.com: https://neurolaunch.com/laundry-therapy/)

82. Kuo, F. E., & Sullivan, W. (2001, July). *Aggression and Violence in the Inner City: Effects of Environment Via Mental Fatigue.* Retrieved October 27, 2024, from JournalsSagePub.com: https://journals.sagepub.com/doi/10.1177/00139160121973124

83. Stevenson, M., Schilhab, T., & Bentsen, P. (2018, August 21). *Attention Restoration Theory II: a systematic review to clarify attention processes affected by exposure to natural environments.* Retrieved October 27, 2024, from PubMed: https://pubmed.ncbi.nlm.nih.gov/30130463/

84. Mayo Clinic . (2024, January 31). *Borderline personality disorder - Symptoms and causes.* Retrieved October 27, 2024, from Mayo Clinic: https://www.mayoclinic.org/diseases-conditions/borderline-personality-disorder/symptoms-causes/syc-20370237

85. Anderson, S. (n.d.). *Welcome to Abandonment Recovery.* Retrieved October 27, 2024, from healing abandonment with Susan Anderson: https://www.abandonment.net/

86. Kropf, J. (2024, October 4). *30 Easy Family Mission Statement Examples & Ideas For 2024.* Retrieved October 31, 2024, from Healthy Happy Impactful: https://healthyhap-

pyimpactful.com/family-mission-statement/
87. Putnam, R. D. (2001). *Bowling Alone: The Collapse and Revival of American Community.* Simon & Schuster.
88. Kotler, S. (2022, May 27). *How 'flow state' can treat anxiety and depression.* Retrieved October 23, 2024, from Big Think: https://bigthink.com/series/explain-it-like-im-smart/flow-state/
89. University of Oregon . (n.d.). *Types of Stress: Positive, Tolerable and Toxic Stress.* Retrieved October 21, 2024, from Types of Stress: Positive, Tolerable and Toxic Stress: https://center.uoregon.edu/StartingStrong/uploads/STARTINGSTRONG2016/HANDOUTS/KEY_49962/TypesofStress.pdf
90. Moog, N., Entringer, S., Rasmussen, J. M., Styner, M., Gilmore, J. H., Kathmann, N., . . . Buss, C. (2017, July 21). *Intergenerational effect of maternal exposure to childhood maltreatment on newborn brain anatomy.* Retrieved from PubMed Central: https://pmc.ncbi.nlm.nih.gov/articles/PMC5723537/
91. Jaffe, D. T. (2020). *Borrowed from Your Grandchildren: The Evolution of 100-Year Family Enterprises.* (D. T. Jaffe (10), Ed.) Wiley.
92. Fraley, R. C. (2018). *A Brief Overview of Adult Attachment Theory and Research | R. Chris Fraley.* Retrieved October 22, 2024, from Psychology Department Labs: https://labs.psychology.illinois.edu/~rcfraley/attachment.htm
93. Komisar, E. (2017). *Being There: Why Prioritizing Motherhood in the First Three Years Matters.* Penguin Publishing Group.
94. Fleck, C. (2024, September 30). *"Mastering the Head Game": 6 Life-Changing Insights from ADHD Gurus.* Retrieved from ADDitude: https://www.additudemag.com/how-to-deal-with-adhd-expert-strategies/

 **RUSCHELLE KHANNA, LCSW** is a clinical psychotherapist, educator, and family advisor who works with individuals and families in the United States and Europe. A member of the Purposeful Planning Institute, she is a licensed clinical social worker with over twenty years experience helping navigate the challenges of health and wealth.

In addition to holding a Masters Degree from Columbia University, Ruschelle holds advanced certificates from NYU in clinical supervision, the NLP Center of NY in clinical hypnosis and Om Factory, NYC as a Registered Yoga Instructor. Ruschelle has meditated since she was 12 years old and has been trained in Transcendental Meditation (TM) through the TM Center in NYC.

She regularly conducts workshops with family businesses and community organizations on the subjects of health, mental health and wealth. She also contributes to publications such as Parenting.com and numerous podcasts on financial therapy and family dynamics.